301 EAST CAPITOL

TALES FROM THE HEART OF THE HILL

– by –

Mary Z. Gray

OVERBECK HISTORY PRESS

Washington, DC • www.OverbeckPress.org

OVERBECK HISTORY PRESS

A project of the Capitol Hill Community Foundation

www.OverbeckPress.org

ISBN-10: 0615543413

ISBN-13: 9780615543413

Library of Congress Control Number: 2011939425

Overbeck History Press, Washington, DC

Front cover photo by John Franzén

Back cover Capitol photo (c. 1917) courtesy Library of Congress

Back cover portrait by Alice Jackson

Printed in the United States of America

First Edition

DEDICATION

To Indigo, Ysabel and Cosmo:
the best great-grandchildren ever.

"WITH GOD, ALL THINGS ARE NOW."

– Henry Alline

CONTENTS

INTRODUCTION

Just north of where the Potomac and the Anacostia Rivers meet, a hill rises above the flat land that surrounds it.

It's an elevation made for signal fires and messages spelled out in puffs of smoke, visible for miles around.

The Nacostin tribe that once inhabited this area could well have used it as a communications center.

And today, the majestic Capitol that now commands these heights is sending out messages by day and night to the neighborhood, the city, the nation and the world: The Union has survived. Democracy is alive and well. The Constitution still works. Hallelujah!

This is not to say that the Congress of the United States, which meets here on Capitol Hill, is flawless and its members are the best the country has to offer – although some are. Nor the worst – although some are.

Our government will never be perfect because it is political (from Greek politikos, "of the citizens"), and nobody is perfect. But the premise as well as the promise of democracy remains intact: Freedom from inherited power; freedom from imposed religion; freedom from ancient tribal feuds; and freedom to establish and practice self-governance by the citizens. A radically new concept for a brave new world. A work in constant progress on Capitol Hill.

"Here the people rule," as Alexander Hamilton put it.

And then there is the other Capitol Hill. A proud neighborhood whose identity flows from the East Front of the Capitol, spilling over to the north and south a few blocks from East Capitol Street, and extending eastward to 14th Street or a bit beyond. Borders can be vague, depending on historical perspective and pride of location.

Here the people live.

And here my people – the Zurhorsts and the Schroeders, the Sheltons and the McGowans – lived for five or more generations. All within ten blocks of each other on Capitol Hill, starting in 1840.

This book is about their lives – myself included – in random moments that have survived in writing or in memory, and their close relationship to both Capitol Hills and the capital city they helped to shape.

CHAPTER 1

IN SESSION

As a child, the first words that I remember being taught to say were, "Now I lay me down to sleep ..."

The second were, "They're in session."

My family lived at 301 East Capitol Street, just two blocks from the Capitol of the whole United States of America.

In winter, when the trees were bare, we had a clear view of that beloved building, just up the street. Even with the trees in full foliage, we had glimpses of the dome or a portico glistening in the sunlight. The East Front of the Capitol was our neighbor. Our friend.

I felt much more tenderly related to it than I did to many of our relatives, like Aunt Arabella, or Cousin Wilbur, who wore white year-round and buttoned his pearl-grey spats over his impeccable white shoes.

In the early 1920s, when I could barely reach our apartment window that framed the dome, I checked every morning to reassure myself that the Capitol was still there. Every night, after the sun had backlit the dome and then sunk behind it, I took one last look before going to bed.

To my delight, when I was about three, I was given a political plum. I got the job of announcing to my parents and five-years-older brother that the Senate and/or House was "in session." Then all four of us would gather, to look up at the East Front. Sometimes Papa knew what law they were voting on.

The signal I watched for was a bright light between the top of the dome and the Statue of Freedom. It's a special light, and different from the floodlights that bathe that great white dome from sunset to sunrise. It comes on only when Congress – one or both branches – is working overtime on the nation's business, after dark.

The light shines from the twelve windows that encircle the small, Grecian-style temple atop the Capitol dome. Twelve Corinthian columns surround the structure. Although it seems tiny seen from below, it's 50 feet high, and it's called a tholos. It's my special part of the whole Capitol.

My political assignment made me feel special. Usually, because of seniority (and gender), Brother got all the plums. He got to run down to Mr. Johnnie's at Fourth and East Capitol and bring home ice cream cones for everybody. He carried them like a bridal bouquet, licking a leak or two that slid down the sides. When it was very hot he ran very fast to get them back before they melted.

He was also the one who paid the paper boy who – before news on radio or TV or the Internet – stood with his latest editions beneath our windows, yelling, "Extra, Extra, Extra, Mussolini Marches on Rome," "Ku Klux Klan Steps Up Violence," "Scopes Convicted in Monkey Trial," "Lindbergh Lands in Paris!"

In addition, Brother could go to matinees at the old Senate Theater around on Pennsylvania Avenue, S.E., where they played mostly "Wild West" movies. He went with Grandpap, my mother's father. "You wouldn't like it," Grandpap would tell me when I begged to go with them. "It gets wild."

It also got wet. The roof leaked. Sometimes when it wasn't even raining. The regulars who attended the shows always carried an umbrella with them, and, I'm told, they would raise it during the movie if it was raining.

My brother, frankly, was a spoiled brat. He tripped me when nobody was looking, called me "Droopy Drawers," "Fatso," and much worse.

After seeing Will Rogers in a vaudeville skit at Poli's Theater, he taught himself the art of rope twirling and lassoing, and played cowboy incessantly. He got me to play the cow. One day he lassoed me around the neck and dragged me up East Capitol Street until one of the men who worked for our business rescued me.

No question, my brother – known to all but me as Snooie – was a rotten, mean little bully.

I adored him. Bully or not, he was my Big Brother. My Hero.

Even though I usually snitched on him ("Tattletale," he'd call out), it was just for the record, in a sense. I never wanted him punished. In the rare times when it seemed imminent that justice would be served, I would plead his case. "He didn't mean to hurt me."

He improved greatly with age, but it took a few years.

Our apartment – we rarely called it home – was on the third floor of a large, rather gracefully designed structure, built pre-Civil War. We lived "over the parlors" of a Capitol Hill business that was proclaimed in elegant gilded lettering on a plate-glass window: "Zurhorst Funeral Home – established in 1868."

My father was the reluctant, third-generation heir to the business, summoned back by his father from the start of a journalism career on a Chicago newspaper. These were the "good old days" when a father's word was law.

"My God, what a way to make a living," my father would wail. "Traffickers in human sorrow – that's all we are."

Papa was a tall, slender, blond *bon vivant*, miscast as an undertaker. He loved fast airplanes, fast cars; he had a 40-foot yacht called "The Greyling," which was no longer with us when I was born. He smoked Havana cigars, jealously loved my mother, and most of the time had a vibrant smile on his face, and too often a "little smile" (liquid) in his hand. "Come, have a 'little smile' with me," he would invite his many men friends or perfect strangers, and they always accepted.

When the "little smiles" were downed closer and closer together – particularly after the burial of a child – Mama would bundle up Brother and me in our coats and send us around the corner to Granny's at 318 A Street, S.E. She was my mother's mother. There were no streets to cross, and Brother was always reminded to "hold Sissy's hand." I was under five, and Brother under ten.

I don't know what either of us was thinking on the way. We didn't speak. Neither of us ever knew why we were being sent to Granny's. We never asked. Maybe we were afraid to know.

We would stay on A Street for an hour or overnight, or sometimes for a week. Occasionally Mama came with us.

When Papa was over whatever it was, he'd come breezing into Granny's, announcing loudly, "I want my wife and family." After passionately embracing Mama, he would swoop Brother and me into his arms and take us all back to our place.

A little ritual of this atonement ceremony was the slipping of a paper cigar ring onto my middle finger. This meant that we were a family again and everything was all right.

The sharpest memory I have of my mother is seeing her at the grand piano in our living room – over the "parlors" – glossy, gypsy-black hair caught in a bun at the back of her head, as she ran her hands over the keyboard without touching a key. There was a funeral going on downstairs, and we must keep silence.

A brilliantly colored fire opal on her right hand seemed to shoot sparks when she was making music, but for now all was quiet. Brother and I, at such times, tiptoed through the living room, the tension palpable. Watching the funeral procession leave was not enough; we had to *know* that everyone was gone before we could make any noise.

Then the phone rang. The maid answered it, and called out, "They gone." The word had come from downstairs.

Mama attacked the keyboard with the rumbling, brooding introduction to "Pace, Pace," from Verdi's *La Forza del Destino*. That first high note of "Pace" (peace!) split the silence like a gun going off. While Mama loosed her professionally trained, glorious soprano voice to plead for "Peace, peace, peace, peace, my God, peace!" Brother and I released our tension by stomping all over the apartment. I never learned to stomp so well as Brother did.

My mother had the voice, the looks and the classical training for a career in music – as a fourth-generation Capitol Hill musician. She lacked only permission from her father and husband to accept the professional offers that came her way. She never got that permission.

So her position was the reverse of Papa's. He was doing the work he loathed because his father ordered him to do it. She was barred from doing the work she loved because her father and husband forbade her to do it.

In the middle of these dramatic dramatis personae, there was me: mousy, straight brown hair and a squint. Nobody seemed to know that I was near-sighted. I often heard, "Smile, Sissy, smile." But a smile plus a squint becomes a grimace, so I didn't smile much.

A younger sister of Granny's, Aunt Gertie, who lived with Granny and Grandpap at 318 A, S.E., worried about the life I was leading as a small child. "Living over the funeral parlors like that can't be good for her," she complained. So she decided to get me away from the morbid surroundings and take me to work with her from time to time.

Aunt Gertie worked as a bookkeeper at Congressional Cemetery.

We would take our lunches in paper bags, and sometimes I took my baby doll in its carriage with me. It was a rather long walk from Third and East Capitol over to the cemetery at 18th and E Streets, S.E., but I didn't mind. I loved going there.

My great-aunt let me toll the bell for funerals as they came through the gate, and that was fun. On a good day there might be three or four funerals to toll for.

When the weather was nice, we would have a picnic near the grave of Pushmataha, a noted Indian chief of the Choctaws. He was known for his diplomacy as well as his warrior skills, and had fought on the side of the U.S. in the War of 1812. When he died in Washington in 1824, he was buried with full military honors.

Some days, when business was slow, we could leave early. That meant we would have time to stop by for a visit with Cousin Willy Shelton, a master stone cutter, who owned a big stone yard near the cemetery, where he would carve names and decorations into gravestones. I was fascinated.

Mama always thanked Aunt Gertie for taking me to Congressional with her. Aunt Gertie usually responded with "It makes a nice change of scenery for the child. We'll go again."

And we did go again, many times. Happy times at the cemetery.

And there were happy times even "over the parlors," despite the lack of children my age to play with. I had my job watching for the light on the Capitol dome, and I had a fully furnished, wall-to-wall carpeted doll's house with curtains made by Granny, inhabited by a whole family of dolls including a maid and butler, who brought to life its four elegant rooms.

I don't remember ever being lonely. From the earliest times I had playmates who were always with me – Mr. and Mrs. Fingernail (my two index fingers) and their eight children. I could talk to them for hours without an audible word.

In fact, the silence of my hobbies suited them perfectly for above the funeral parlors.

The considerable space in front of our building at the corner of East Capitol and Third Street was paved over to form a wide expanse of sidewalk, and there was no back yard, so I couldn't be told to "go outside and play." There were no preschools, play dates or pools to go to, and the closest thing to a neighborhood playground was Lincoln Park – a green square featuring a statue of Lincoln freeing a slave – several blocks down East Capitol Street from us. The sculpture of noted educator Mary McLeod Bethune romping with pre-schoolers hadn't arrived yet.

We had a maid called Toodie, and she sometimes took me down to Lincoln Park.

She had several children of her own, even though she seemed much like a child herself – small, playful, timid. She was with us for only a year or so.

Who took care of Toodie's children? She rarely mentioned her children, never calling them by name. One day I asked her who took care of her kids when she worked, and she muttered that the BYPU (Baptists Young People's Union) helped out. I was asking not out of concern, but because I was wondering if she would bring some with her for me to play with. But I didn't follow through with the idea. A few days later, I found her scrubbing the kitchen sink, softly sobbing.

As she caught sight of me, she tried to disguise the sobs by singing the words to a modern hymn of praise that I had heard broadcast from an inner-city church on Sundays. She often spoke of the preacher, Elder Solomon Lightfoot Michaux.

"Happy am I," goes the lilting tune. "Oh, yes, I'm happy." Tears were streaming down her face.

Disturbed, I asked Mama what was wrong with Toodie. "She's crying," I said.

Mama drew me to her and said not to bother Toodie with questions right now. She looked almost as sad as Toodie. With a deep sigh, she whispered, "She's going to have another baby."

The maid we had briefly, after Toodie, left an indelible mark on my memory. She was tall and slim, with a back as straight as that of an African princess wearing a crown atop that tightly curled hair. Her name was Olivia Birdsong.

She hadn't been with us very long before I found her in the kitchen one day with her head resting on her arm laid across the countertop.

Little snoop that I was, I told Granny, who went into the kitchen and asked if she didn't have work to do. With no emotion showing, Olivia Birdsong reported that she had cleaned the apartment, made the beds, taken out the trash and prepared the vegetables for dinner. There was nothing further to do until dinner time.

301 East Capitol. Our third floor apartment, above the family business,
looked out on the U.S. Capitol.

My mother Edwinetta, the singer.

My father, before the mustache.

Papa (in straw hat) and a friend with Brother and me.

"Well," said Granny, "you're not being paid to sleep. Find something to do."

Her expression unchanged, Olivia Birdsong slowly rose, removed her purse and coat from the wall hook and walked out the door. She didn't even ask for the pay she was due.

Young as I was, I felt a kind of thrill at this class act. And she never said a word. It was awesome.

"Well, I never," said Granny in a shocked whisper.

Osceola May Harper – Oscie (Ohsee) – answered an ad my mother had placed in the *Post* for a maid to cook, clean and look after a small child. Seven days a week, half days Thursday and Sunday. Salary: $7 a week.

She had straight black hair and a sassy attitude that said, "I'll go by your rules, but I have my rules, too. And don't mess with me."

Mama asked if Osceola was an Indian name. Oscie shrugged. "My mother say he was a Indian chief. But what do she know?"

Switching the subject to food, Mama asked if she could cook such things as venison, steak and kidney pie and rabbit stew. Oscie dropped her jaw. "Y'all eat rabbit?" She let out a snort. "I knows *you* sick," she hooted.

In the stunned silence, Oscie recovered her dignity, drew herself up to her full five feet tall and proclaimed, "Sure I can cook those things if that's what you want. I can learn to cook anything. Just try me."

"All right, Oscie, I'll try you," said Mama.

"You mean I got the job?" asked Oscie, who hugged herself with joy and disbelief. "I knows *you* sick!"

We came to understand that "I knows *you* sick" was an all-purpose expression that could mean something like the much later high five, or "You crazy," or even embarrassment when she was being complimented on her superb cooking.

Her shocking comment meant no harm nor disrespect. But I was glad that Granny hadn't interviewed Oscie or, with the first "I knows *you* sick" she would have been out the door.

When Mama told Granny the next day that she had hired a new maid, Granny asked what she was like.

"Spunky," said Mama.

"I'm not sure spunk is a quality I'd want in a maid," Granny offered.

"She'll be fine," Mama said, giving me a conspiratorial smile. "And Sissy likes her. I could tell."

For the first time in my life, I felt that my opinion mattered. And Mama and I were acting together over Granny's better judgment.

I wasn't to feel so grown up again until my sophomore year in college when a young English professor explained to the class a literary reference to the sexual connotations of a mandrake root.

On one of our earliest expeditions, Oscie and I walked down to the Smithsonian Museum of Natural History on the Mall. (We had streetcar fare to ride home.) As we wandered through the museum, Oscie suddenly let out a war whoop that brought the guards running. She had encountered a gigantic bust of Osceola, Chief of the Seminoles. Here was the proof – in a sense – that her mother had told her the truth, and that she really did have Indian blood. She was a little less of a skeptic on a lot of things after that revelation.

Oscie and I usually didn't stray far from home when we began to explore our world. Why go far afield when within three or four blocks there at the heart of Capitol Hill we had the Capitol of the United States, the Library of Congress, Mr. Johnnie's Ice Cream and Candy Store, Grubb's Pharmacy, Sherrill's Bakery and Restaurant, McPhee's Men's Haberdashery, at least four churches, one school, four doctors, a barbershop, two corner grocery stores, two delicatessens, a dentist, a milliner, a leaky movie theater, Providence Hospital, four undertakers and Santa Claus?

There were also a few banks and some Donohoe businesses (real estate or whatever) but they were out of our league and we ignored them. As for 203 Third Street, S.E., that was off-limits, of course. I didn't know why.

All of these conveniences and necessities were in a residential neighborhood. To Oscie and me they were just there, part of the day's outing. Except for Santa Claus. He was special. And he was the real thing.

Grown-ups called him "old Mr. Brodt," but Oscie and I knew better. He had real snow-white hair and a real snow-white beard that was fluffy and just right – not one of those fake, stupid curly things that make-believe Santa Clauses wear. He had a round little belly, and a radiant smile, and he loved children. Best of all, he never said that idiotic "Ho, ho, ho."

He lived just three or four doors down Third Street from us. Having him there was like having elves in the attic, or finding a talking rabbit among the Easter eggs. Our neighborhood's enchanting secret.

For every year of my childhood that I remember, Mr. Brodt was Santa Claus at Woodward & Lothrop's, our favorite department store, at Eleventh and F Streets, N.W. Only "Woodies" would have the *real* Santa Claus.

When Brother (in his younger years) and I visited Santa in the store at Christmas time, we got special hugs and winks. And we had little chats in his front yard all through the year. And sometimes a peppermint.

I'm still sure that *our* Santa Claus was the real one. He was.

There was no question about the reality of the Capitol building up the street. I saw it several times a day – but usually from our west window. Oscie brought it into my life, up close. Its lawn became my playground.

Oscie and I first explored the East Front, because that was our side of the Capitol. I was free to scamper all over the "street furniture" – mainly the endless, stone seat-walls that the Capitol's premier landscape architect Frederick Law Olmsted called "a parapet of pierced stonework formed with a back." I climbed on these massive benches daringly – if Oscie held my hand.

We could only wonder at some strange, ungainly structures opposite the Capitol's front steps. They were unclimbable and utterly useless, as far as we could tell. They were also stone, and oval-shaped. Even the matching ornamental stonework on the base of the street lights baffled us. They weren't even pretty. We soon grew tired of them and decided to "go around back."

Wait ... wait just a moment. Paths are about to cross.

Time is bending at the East Front of the Capitol. They

can't see each other – the little girl and the young bandsman with the wavy hair and the luxuriant mustache – but
they are both there, in God's time. Eternal time. When
all things are NOW. Real time, as when we see stars in
the night sky that disappeared into a black hole eons ago.
Yet they still glow. The calendar of the musician says it
is March 4, 1861 – the day of Abraham Lincoln's first
inauguration.

The classically trained cornetist with the United
States Marine Band is ... was ... will be ... my maternal
great-grandfather. His name is August Wilhelm Schroeder.

Despite the tension that surrounds him, he appears
calm, poised.

All around the East Front of the Capitol, sharpshooters stand at the ready. A crowd is gathering at a wooden
platform built over the east steps to the main entrance. It's
guarded by a solid line of soldiers armed with bayonets.

Except for a few whiskey-soaked hecklers shouting,
"Hurrah for Jeff Davis," or scratching themselves like apes
and making rude gestures, it's a quiet crowd – quiet but
tense. Men are making bets on the hour when the incoming
President will be shot. Most of the dignitaries in attendance
are armed.

The secessionists have seceded from the House and
Senate, have taken the train down south to home. But loyal
southerners are still present, not just across the Potomac
in Virginia, but also right here in front of the Capitol and
throughout the city. They're even mingling on the speaker's platform, where there's much shuffling about to avoid
an improper seatmate.

A bomb squad occupies the space under the platform, following one of many bomb threats. Sharpshooters fill the Capitol porticos and east windows, as well as rooftops on the boardinghouse across the street.

When a gust of wind sends a spectator's stovepipe hat sailing into the air, instantly the sharpshooters leap into action, muskets at the ready. Is this the long-awaited signal for the war to begin? Has the time come for the promised assassinations?

When nothing happens, the people realize that it was just a hat blowing in the wind, and much of the tension drains away.

After a few preliminaries, Mr. Lincoln steps up to the small table at the front of the stage. Hisses and catcalls erupt, along with shouts of "Orangutan," and "Ignoramus" as several men and women down front turn their backs on him – a reminder of the closed shutters on homes and businesses that lined his route up Pennsylvania Avenue from the Willard Hotel for the swearing-in ceremony at the Capitol. Anything to show their contempt.

He ignores the insults – what choice does he have? – removes his stovepipe hat and looks around helplessly for some place to put it, out of the wind. Eventually a friend takes it from him.

In reversal of traditional order, he gives his inaugural address first, followed by the swearing-in. Chief Justice Roger Brooke Taney is to administer the oath of office. He's the Chief Justice responsible for the Dred Scott decision, which denied freedom to a former slave living in a free state. In fact, Chief Justice Taney held that the Constitution of the United States gave no civil rights or legal protections to Negroes.

Lincoln had pronounced this ruling "a burlesque upon judicial decisions." Now he is about to come face to face with this man who represents the Southern majority on the Supreme Court – to be sworn in by him.

Justice Taney, 83 and ill, looks like a "galvanized corpse," according to a reporter covering the event.

The swearing-in passes without incident. In fact, seeing Mr. Lincoln for the first time and hearing him speak seems to have had a salutary effect upon some in the crowd. They can now judge him for themselves, rather than through the cartoonists and his detractors. They see he's no fool. Some in the audience – especially women – find him strangely appealing, to their surprise. He has that special attraction of vulnerability coupled with masculine strength.

His supporters on the platform gather to shake his hand. To have the ordeal almost over is a welcome moment. Ready to celebrate that moment, the United States Marine Band Master Francis Maria Scala steps forward to announce that the band will now play a new composition, titled "Union March," written in honor of this occasion by Scala himself, and dedicated to "Mrs. President Lincoln."

There are a few displeased murmurings from across a wide political spectrum in the audience – Union sympathizers who think Mrs. Lincoln is a Confederate spy, Southern loyalists who accuse the Southern belle from Kentucky of being a turncoat, and the rabble-rousers who welcome every opportunity to humiliate Abraham Lincoln.

It turns out to be a minor protest, and the people quiet down to listen to the music ... and to feast their eyes on the band members, resplendent in their scarlet tunics glistening with gold braid, topping sky blue trousers.

Notice especially the one now raising the cornet to his lips. Handsome, isn't he?

As soon as we made the turn that brought us "around back" of the Capitol, I broke loose from Oscie's hand and took off. Ahead of me and on all sides was an ocean of lush, green grass, shadowed in part by billowy trees with broad, shiny leaves. Then there were squat, exotic trees with lacey leaves that trembled as if frightened. And mid-sized trees with tops like umbrellas. And some stretches of wide-open, sunlit lawn with no trees at all.

Almost every tree had a plaque on it, giving it a name. We couldn't read these nameplates, but, nevertheless, they made each tree something special and unique.

And there was freedom in all directions. I could go where I fancied, and still be safely within Oscie's purview.

Who could have known that this wonderland had been hiding all the time, behind the Capitol?

Except that it wasn't really "behind the Capitol," I learned many years later. The Capitol has no behind. It has an East Front and a West Front. Each equally impressive and grand.

To me, it became my playground, my front yard, my back yard, my own special place.

In my under-five, center-of-the-universe mentality, these wondrous trees and dappled green lawns existed just for Oscie and me. The bushes were for our hide-and-go-seek games. We rarely ever saw anybody else there. Oh, there were a few other people on the paths, walking briskly and looking straight ahead – or down the hill, where, we figured, they worked. We let them pass through our territory, but we knew it didn't belong to them as it belonged to us.

Most of these intruders used the broad walkways that wander through the lawn, but occasionally a few took the long, shallow flights of stairs that descended the hill.

Nobody used those stairs the way I did, though.

The trick was to go down in a leisurely way, then almost at the foot of them – with Oscie in pursuit – dart over the wall and start running. Never give a clue as to which direction you'll take, just so you confuse Oscie when she runs after you. These races confused the squirrels, too, and started them scampering all over the lawn. It was fun.

At one point, I learned how to stand perfectly still on a path, holding a peanut in my hand, while making a clicking noise with my tongue. Suddenly, from the upper branches of the trees, squirrels appeared on the trunks, then tentatively approached, each with a different degree of timidity – or bravado. The bold ones crept close. Others – always the same ones – kept their distance. They were the ones I favored with a tossed peanut.

Another drama that still plays out regularly on the grounds of the West Front is the late summer Harvest of the Horse Chestnuts – those designer-perfect, reddish mahogany, smooth-as-polished-marble horse chestnuts. You don't just hold this nut-like seed (not really a nut) from Constantinople in your hand; you fondle it, rub its slippery surface with your thumb, and delight in the tactile pleasure.

21

Around the end of August or early September, as I remember, thousands of horse chestnuts covered the pathways through the Capitol's "back yard." I packed my pockets with them to bring home as gifts. (I don't think the recipients were as enamored with them as I was, but I tried to teach anyone who would listen – and feel – what marvels they were.)

When Oscie and I tired of chasing squirrels and each other, we found sanctuary and a welcoming cool haven in our favorite spot in all the world at the time – the "secret grotto." Hidden among low-spreading trees and bushes in a hillside of the west lawn, it was designed as a "summerhouse" to refresh and delight the passerby. Its creator was that superb landscape architect, Frederick Law Olmsted, who was responsible for the Capitol grounds as well as Central Park in New York City.

There is a drinking fountain in the hexagonal summerhouse. A tiled, ivy-covered roof partially covers the seats on either side of the fountain. (Olmsted planted the original ivy himself.) The seats are bluestone, and the flooring – now cement – used to be a rough brick. Horses were allowed to get a cool drink at the fountain until a few sober minds deemed it unsanitary to let humans and animals slurp at the same water jet.

Olmsted wanted this lovely sanctuary to merge into the low hillside and be "lost to view." He succeeded.

Descend a few steps from the walkway, and enter a summer haven that seems about ten degrees cooler than the surrounding grounds. And suddenly, all around is the sound of running water. Its source is in a rocky cave in the northeast wall of the summerhouse – a grotto – filled with rocks and ferns and mosses and other wet things and wild things, all forming the setting for a hillside spring.

It's a magic place.

When winter was drawing near and the summerhouse was closed off behind a huge iron gate, our interest shifted to the inside of the Capitol. It was time to go in.

I made this suggestion to Oscie one day when we found we were locked out of our grotto and heard no sound from the spring. (The pipe that carried the spring water from near Soldiers' Home, about three miles north, had been turned off for the winter.)

"Go inside the Capitol?" shrieked Oscie. "I knows *you* sick. We not supposed to go *in* there, you and me."

I badgered her until she agreed, reluctantly, to take a peep.

We entered inch by inch, through the street level arches of the East Front. Oscie reverted to her Seminole ancestry as she crept through the corridors like a young brave stalking prey in a forest – with me a few paces behind. On tiptoe, God knows why.

She would motion for me to stay back as she scouted a few feet ahead, heel to toe, without making a sound.

She'd stick her head far out around corners, looking in all directions until it was safe to proceed. Then she'd motion for me to join her.

Early on, Oscie set the rules: No running, no opening any doors or taking any elevators. There was a lot of space to cover in that vast building without opening doors. And we saw a lot of it – all in that stealthy way, as if we would meet someone any minute who would throw us out. I never knew what she feared we would encounter. Maybe she didn't know either, but she was never convinced that it was all right for us to be there.

Except in the Rotunda, we didn't look up much. I have no memories of elaborate frescoed ceilings along the richly decorated corridors, nor of any artwork on the walls, with the exception of the gigantic painting over one of the marble stairways labeled "Westward the Course of Empire Takes Its Way."

The statues in Statuary Hall were overwhelming, and a little intimidating to a small child. Yet I enjoyed going there – especially the trick spot for whispering.

Oscie and I learned a lot from attaching ourselves to the fringes of tour groups, and listening to tour guides. We had fun, after the tours cleared out, standing in the spot where you can whisper and be heard all the way across that great space – but only in the right spot and not in between.

"I knows *you* sick!" Oscie would whisper, and I'd giggle, knowing no one else could hear us.

We found the narrow, curving, stone stairway where, it is said, an invading British soldier was shot in the War of 1812. Or was it a brash reporter who shot it out with ... somebody ... on those steps? We shivered, appropriately, when we found the "blood spots" that won't scrub off.

One day, deep in the Capitol's lower levels, we came across a room with iron bars that protected a long stand draped in funereal black. This was the catafalque that had held Lincoln's body when he lay in state in the rotunda, I learned many years later.

As Oscie and I skidded happily across the marble floors, we were deaf to the sounds of suffering, the muted cries and moans that filled the rotunda and every available foot of floor space in the building.

Outside, where we had been scampering over well groomed lawns, deep ruts were being cut into the side of the hill by ox carts and horse-drawn wagons bearing bodies, alive and dead. Stacks of them.

It is mid-September, 1862. In the parallel universe Oscie and I were in, it was 1924.

The air around the Capitol is heated and still – as if holding its breath in shock at the news.

Twelve thousand four hundred Federal casualties on September 17, just two days ago, at the Battle of Antietam in nearby Maryland. The bloodiest day of the Civil War.

A few days earlier, the toll was *sixteen thousand* casualties among Union soldiers within 48 hours of fighting, at the Second Battle of Bull Run.

The military strategists have disastrously underestimated the strength of the Southern army. Now the military and civilian leaders of the country are grossly unprepared for the tragic results. All rooms that can be spared in the Capitol building – and any other sizable spaces in the city, including 301 East Capitol – have been commandeered to house the maimed and the dying. Over 1,500 cots fill the Capitol, with thousands more casualties pouring into the city up Pennsylvania Avenue and other dusty paths on wagons and on foot, headed for the Capitol, turning the rough roads red with blood behind them.

Battle-scarred men are roaming the Capitol grounds, bloody, unwashed, unpaid for months, pleading for justice – and promises to be kept – with anyone who will listen.

These walking wounded are frightened and angry. And every one of them is still carrying the gun issued to the men of the Grand Army of the Potomac. Many have been drinking. It's an explosive situation.

And it's made more poignant by the presence of young wives of the soldiers (some have brought their children with them) seeking wounded husbands – or their bodies.

Across from Capitol Plaza, a slender, blue-eyed man with a beard leaves his rooming house on First Street and enters the swarming grounds of the East Front. Many approach him because his height makes him appear to be someone in authority. He's over six feet tall. Close to seven in his stovepipe hat.

Many times, he explains sorrowfully that he can do nothing to help – nothing beyond what he is already doing.

Better not dwell on the nature of his business.

He, too, was at Antietam. He returned to the city with the first wagon train of wounded Union veterans.

He comes to this spot early each morning, and often through the day, entering the building through a lower-level, arched doorway, and comes out again an hour or so later, leading a solemn procession of men carrying wooden coffins. They place the coffins on wagons that had arrived within the hour, weighted down with wounded men desperate to fill the cots so recently vacated.

This is but one of many trips he will make today to the makeshift, unlikely hospital/morgue/Capitol. As he waits for the next human cargo, he visits with the workmen sweating it out in tents spread across the East Front, following President Lincoln's order that the building of the Capitol continue, as a symbol that the Union – the United States of America – still endures.

Some are finishing the enormous columns for the porticos; others are carving acanthus leaves to grace the capitals atop the columns.

Carefully avoiding the steaming mounds of droppings from horse and mule and ox befouling the Capitol's busy East Front, this imposing figure heads back to his rooming house across First Street in hopes of at least one quick meal on this unhappy day.

If he takes time to glance two blocks down East Capitol Street, he will see a stately, handsome building that, in a few years, will be his own. And his son's, and his son's, and his son's, and *his* son's – if he wants it. It's 301 East Capitol.

His name is Charles Frederick Zurhorst, who is already ... but not yet (in the eternal NOW of cosmic time) ... my paternal great-grandfather.

CHAPTER 2

THE NEIGHBORHOOD

Sometimes Oscie and I would go home from the Capitol by way of the Neptune fountain in front of the Library of Congress. I thought it was fascinating, but disturbing. The horses seemed writhing in agony and doing their best to throw off those girls riding bareback.

Oscie looked at it wryly, asking one day, "Why they spittin' like that? Those men and the turtles and the snakes, all spittin'."

I had often wondered the same thing when Mama had brought me here, but hadn't asked. Jets of water splashed all over the active figures, and made their bodies shine.

Now Oscie's eyes narrowed. Apparently, she hadn't looked at the magnificently sculpted group in depth before.

"I don't think you s'posed to be here," she said, grabbing my elbow.

"Why not?" I asked.

"Those people got no clothes on," she said, shaking her head in disapproval. "And that old man with the beard [Neptune] sittin' on that rock. He naked as a jaybird." She steered me away. "Come on, we gotta get outta here." And she took me home.

Mama explained that it was all right to look at that group of naked people because they were statues, and it was art.

"Humph," commented Oscie. "I knows *you* sick."

∞

The shops along Pennsylvania Avenue, S.E., near Third and Fourth drew us like a magnet, and sometimes got us into trouble. Ever since the time I had disgraced us with the money-lending scheme, Oscie was fearful in that part of our neighborhood.

As we drew near Sherrill's Bakery that day, I could smell the luscious French apple cake baking, and I told Oscie we should buy one and take it home for dinner. "Where you gonna get the money?" she asked. Neither of us had any.

Down the street I saw the haberdashery store where Papa got some of his clothes, and it gave me an idea. "We'll charge it," I said. I knew Papa had a charge account there, but I wasn't sure about having one at Sherrill's.

"I knows *you* sick," sniffed Oscie. "How you gonna do that?"

I explained that I would ask Mr. Tune or Mr. McPhee (as I recall their names), the two canny Scotsmen who ran the haberdashery store, to charge $1.00 to Papa's account, and give us the cash, which we would take to Sherrill's to buy the cake.

Oscie would have no part of the scheme. "You can't do that, girl. You crazy. You gonna get us in trouble. I'm not goin' in there with you."

So I went in alone. I didn't know Mr. Tune from Mr. McPhee, but one of them was alone in the shop when I explained my plan.

Although the only exact quote that stays with me is, "What's a poor wee thing like you doin' out alone?" I got the message very clearly that there was no chance of getting a penny from Mr. Tune. Or Mr. McPhee. Or any other merchant on "the Avenue."

When I protested that I wasn't alone, that Oscie was waiting for me on the sidewalk, he looked out and saw her, and said, "Did she put you up to this?"

That's when the haggis hit the hat rack. I began pummeling him, yelling, "Don't you dare say Oscie put me up to it. It's not her fault. She told me not to do it. Don't you blame Oscie."

I quickly left the shop, and Oscie and I ran home as fast as we could. Papa told me to steer clear of such schemes, and saw to it that we always had a dollar with us in the future.

It was that dollar and Sherrill's again that brought us more trouble. One day as we were passing Sherrill's, I suggested that we go into the restaurant section and have some peach pie. It was August, and there is nothing to match fresh peach pie.

We had the money to pay for two pieces.

Again, from Oscie, "I knows *you* sick. I can't go in Sherrill's and sit down at a table and eat a piece of pie." She was recoiling as I neared the door.

"Why not? Don't you like peach pie?"

"Sure I like peach pie, but you know I can't go in there and eat it." She looked frightened.

"Come on, Oscie. I can pay for it," I cajoled.

"I'm goin' home," she said. "You comin' with me?" And she started slowly walking up the street.

When we got home, I told Mama about what had happened. "Tell her she can go into Sherrill's," I said. "You tell her."

"No, she can't go into Sherrill's to eat," Mama said softly. "Oscie's right. You should have listened to her."

"Why not? What's wrong with Oscie?"

"There is nothing wrong with Oscie. That's just the way things are. There are certain places colored people can't go. That's just the way it is."

"But it's not fair," I persisted. "Can't you do something to stop that?"

"No, it's not fair. But I can't do anything about it."

And that's the way it was on Capitol Hill – and throughout most of the country – in the 1920s.

After that time, I didn't suggest that Oscie go inside any building, unless I was sure it was all right. I didn't understand then; I don't understand now.

We explored a lot of territory within a few blocks of home. Sometimes we went as far as the old Providence Hospital, past Providence Square, down Third Street, S.E.

I loved to poke into a cavernous barn-like shed off of Third Street, across a large park from the hospital. The dilapidated, dark old building, then empty, used to be a livery stable. (I found out later in life that it had been run by my Grandfather Zurhorst.)

There were bits of hay on the floor and the lingering smell of horse droppings in the air. We didn't go in, just hovered around the wide entrance.

And, of course, on the way down Third, we always crossed the street to keep from passing right in front of 203. We gave that huge stone and brick house a wide berth. Mama or Papa never told us not to go close to 203. We just knew instinctively. It would take me many years to unravel the mystery.

CHAPTER 3

THE PARLORS

"What was it like – living over the funeral parlors? Was it spooky?" Familiar questions to the undertaker's daughter.

Yes, it was spooky. Sometimes.

The high-pitched, wailing whistle that often woke us in the middle of the night set the stage for ghostly drama.

I don't know why we couldn't have had a front doorbell, as most people had. But we weren't most people; we were the undertaker's family, so we had a strange contraption at the front entrance of the funeral parlors that allowed us to speak to those poor souls who had been dispatched in the dark of night to tell the undertaker that his services were needed.

We called this device a speaker's tube. It was set into the doorframe of the corner entrance, directly facing Third and East Capitol. The other end of the tube opened into our third-floor apartment.

The messenger would whistle loudly into the tube. Then Papa would get out of bed, and whistle down the tube, followed by an assurance that he was on his way. And off he'd go, in slippers, robe and pajamas.

We had telephones in the Twenties. Why did someone have to come in person to request the undertaker's aid? And why this archaic instrument at the front door?

Old habits die hard. (I cringe as I write these words.) In our business, certain words like "die" aren't used lightly.

At least once, the speaker's tube was used to trick my father. The shrill whistle sounded, and Papa answered the call, as usual. He opened the door to a whiskery face, weaving unsteadily in the darkness. The man ordered a hearse to come to his house and pick up his nagging wife – who was very much alive.

Although I never saw any real ghosts, there were some strange sounds that Mama found disturbing. We learned of her fears one morning at breakfast.

"Did any family members stay with the body last night?" she asked Papa. Occasionally some did keep vigil by the casket. But Papa denied that anybody had spent the night.

She insisted that she had heard moans or soft weeping. Papa said he hadn't heard a thing.

But the sounds continued, with the added mystery of demitasse spoons disappearing from the silver chest in the dining room.

Then Mama began to hear moans during the daylight hours, and, on counting the demitasse spoons yet again, found two more to be missing. What had been a ghost story was turning into a crime scene, and Mama suspected Papa was the criminal – although she couldn't figure out what the crime was.

Under duress, he confessed. He hadn't been sure that she would approve, so, under cover of darkness, he had brought in through the back of the building several crates of pigeons. He was planning to race them. It was their cooing that Mama had heard. While she was out one day, he had built a pigeon coop on the rear of the building.

And what of the strange case of the disappearing spoons?

Papa had been using them to feed the baby pigeons, the squabs.

After much discussion the two of them reached an agreement; Papa could keep the pigeons if he would return Mama's spoons.

Eventually, the pigeon population decreased to zero – due to taking a wrong turn or falling off the perch or whatever – but two spaces in the silver chest remained forever empty.

Ten years or so after the pigeon mystery, frightening sounds shook up the neighborhood.

One fine spring day, with no body in the parlors, and no school because it was Saturday, I was playing my mother's operatic records on the Victrola, as I browsed through the dog-eared *Victor Book of the Opera*.

While others of my age dreamed of falling down the rabbit hole with Alice, I envisioned splitting a bottle of Manzanilla with my friend Lilas Pastia, down near the ramparts of Seville. Move over, Carmen.

My Peter Rabbit was Enrico Caruso. My Jemima Puddleduck was the golden-voiced Amelita Galli-Curci.

After listening to dozens of Italian opera classics sung by the most glorious voices God ever made (most of them dead by the time I heard their records), I had a terrible urge to share this beauty with the world.

So I threw open a back window, and, in full voice, I filled the air over the alley.

"Je suis Titania," I loudly proclaimed. "Je suis Titania, la blonde … fille de l'air." With tendons and vocal innocence stretched to the limit, I strained to imitate Galli-Curci's pure coloratura soaring effortlessly to heights few voices can reach. Especially mine, with my off-key, untrained, alto vocal cords. But I tried.

When the trills and cadenzas overwhelmed me, I slipped into something more comfortable – the deep, full-throated contralto of Madame Schumann-Heink as Azucena begging her son, Enrico Caruso (of course), to come home to our mountains, located somewhere in *Il Trovatore*. I sang Caruso's part, too.

No prima donna at the Met or La Scala ever took on the solo arias, duets, quartets, sextets and even full choruses that I tackled single-voiced.

Since I knew no Italian and very little French, I sang the lyrics phonetically and in short spurts. There is a phrase, for example, in *Traviata*, last act duet, that I hear as, "Ray pompom parenpweet." Then it repeats maybe an octave lower, "Ray pompom parenpweet." I don't want to know what it really is; I prefer my version.

After demolishing the quartet from *Rigoletto* (Caruso, Galli-Curci and two others), I tore into the sextet from *Lucia*, competing now with Caruso, Galli-Curci and *four* others, each of whom seemed to be elbowing each other to get closest to the microphone. (The English title of the piece is "What Restrains Me?")

Right in the middle of the sextet when everybody's going full speed ahead and the coloratura is gliding in over the heads of all of them, there was a frantic knock at the apartment door.

Two of the men from the office downstairs stood there, with a neighbor from Third Street.

"What's wrong? Is anybody hurt?" The men were shouting over each other.

"Was somebody attacked?"

"Should we get the police?"

The man from Third Street said his wife had first heard "the screaming," and thought it was coming from the alley. She had asked him to go see if he could help. He told us that three or four others had gathered in the alley to see what was going on. And one man who was walking his dog had said that the dog, "on hearing the dreadful screeching," began to howl, and then had run into an open garage and was still too frightened to come out.

They had traced the sounds to our building, but, strangely enough, the men downstairs hadn't heard me half so clearly as those in the back alley. All of them were disgustingly amused to find it was me, singing.

And that was when I decided to become a writer.

The building itself had a ghostly aura, especially near the funeral parlors. (That space has been reborn with all-new walls and halls more suited to its new life. The exterior remains intact, its fine architectural details enhanced by the tender care of expert restorers.)

The most distinguishing feature of the bulky, white brick structure is at its northwest corner: The sharp edge of the building has been sliced off, leaving a recessed corner at first-floor level, graced by double doors with glass panels.

A single column appears to support the overhang of the two upper stories.

The double doors originally opened into a large reception room, with a very high ceiling and a highly polished parquet floor. Against the back wall, a wide curving stairway swept up to the viewing rooms – funeral parlors – on the second floor. The stairs

were carpeted in a muted magenta which made an elegant statement against the dark mahogany railings.

I used to dream that I was flying like Peter Pan over these stairs,
and hovering just under the ceiling. Mama told the doctor about my
nocturnal flights, and he said I had been eating too many potatoes.
But he got it all wrong.

My dreams of flying weren't a *symptom*; they were just my
dreams. Grown-ups are so dense.

This reception room with its beautiful staircase was the only
part of the building that attracted me – unless you can count the
incomparable view of the Capitol out of our third-floor windows.

The three-story, white-painted red brick funeral home appeared
less boxy than it might have were it not for the large, plate glass
windows at first-floor level. At regular intervals – every few
months, it seemed – a man came by and re-gilded the Old English
lettering on these windows: Zurhorst Funeral Home, Established in
1868. He did the lettering by hand, and it was a work of art.

On the first floor were the reception room, office, and at the
back, a huge storage space and cement-floored embalming room,
with a drain in the floor.

The second floor held the funeral parlors and casket display
rooms, and most of the third floor was our family's apartment.

Another apartment in the building faced Third Street, and
spanned two floors. In the Twenties, the manager of the business and his family lived there; my brother and his wife and son
occupied it in the early Thirties.

It was also occupied by large rats.

We didn't have rats in our apartment. We had mice.

They frightened me almost as much as the unseen ghosts did.

And where did we encounter the ghosts? Nowhere, actually. And yet, at that dark door at the *back* of the parlors, on a long passageway to our flat, there was a … *something* … that turned my hands a mottled blue and quivery with cold.

Our quarters had a separate street-level entrance, next to the business office, facing East Capitol Street. The first flight of stairs were scary only when I anticipated passing that ghostly door. It was on the long landing that led to the final steps up to the apartment. With only one dusty window, that part of the hall was dim, with moving shadows formed vaguely by street lights at night and by an oblique northern sunlight by day.

The shadows sometimes gave the effect that the door was slowly … ever so slowly … opening. Just a crack. One night I was sure I heard a rusty hinge creak.

Was someone …?

I never hung around long enough to investigate. I would tear past that ominous spot and speed up the last flight as if I were being chased. Was I?

Maybe I would have been less anxious if I had opened that door and walked into the casket display room that it led to. See – there's nothing there. Fred or Lee, from downstairs, would have walked me through, but I never had the nerve to ask them.

It goes without saying that the embalming room on the ground floor was another threat to sanity. But I never remotely considered entering there.

Those last steps to our flat were terribly, dangerously steep, with an insanely placed window at the base. Its bottom sill was even with the first step.

Family lore has it that a grocery boy fell the length of the stairway, through the window and down to the brick sidewalk, one floor below.

Nobody could verify this story. I think somebody made it up.

Sounds like Brother.

Although it could have happened.

The cruel, cramped stairs came straight up (from the window), and made a sharp turn at the top, where the door to our flat led into a thin hallway.

The first room to greet visitors and inhabitants was the bathroom, then the tiny kitchen, followed by a space that was, from time to time, living room, dining room or bedroom, depending on the latest room plan.

In a futile attempt to get more space, we kept renaming the rooms according to their function, but of course, there was just so much square footage and no more, no matter what we called each room. My mother was not always practical. She was a singer.

Usually, this middle area served as a dining room, which was a logical plan, since it was next to the kitchen. But sometimes it was a bedroom. I have no memory of it except for one time when I could see Brother running around the room, yelling, "No, it tastes bad!"

Mama and Papa were chasing him, with Mama holding a medicine bottle and Papa a spoon. I could see this tableau through the bars of a crib, a memory feat that seems remarkable, considering the fact that I must have been so very young at the time.

Or maybe we were short of beds and I was crammed into a crib well past my time.

Brother, my hero, and me.

It was a rare moment when Brother put me on a pedestal.

Or maybe the whole thing exists only in my imagination. Whatever was going on was taking place in that middle room, as I recall it. I really don't think I made it up.

And – I wasn't going to tell this, but I changed my mind – to show Brother that the medicine didn't taste bad at all, I was given a dose. Which I spat out all over the blanket. Served them right.

When we were using this central room as a bedroom, the only acceptable way to reach the large living room beyond it was through a narrow hall at the side of the living quarters.

One day, as we were leaving for summer vacation, we cleared out the fish tanks that lined the corridor. We left them empty – we thought – except for what we took for dead tadpoles clinging to the sides of the tanks.

The night we returned for the start of the school year, we heard plopping sounds around the apartment, but we didn't see anything until Brother emerged from the hallway festooned with little green creatures, leaping and chirping all over him. The inert tadpoles had morphed into full-grown frogs.

No, we didn't have frog legs for dinner. Mama called one of the men downstairs and he took care of them.

(It seems to me now that we took advantage of "the men downstairs," who had been hired to tend to dead bodies of people, not live frogs or mice or us.)

We managed to squeeze a bit more space out of the old building by adding an annex to the back, facing the one-car garages in the alley. Now we had a sleeping porch, which at some time became a dining room – with a false floor the entire length and width of the room. It gave us a crawl space about three feet deep, entered through a rug-covered trap door.

This was a secret place where my grandmother could hide her homemade – and illegal – blackberry wine.

She made it at our summer house, and when we transported it up to Washington, everybody in the car had been taught how to toss the sealed jugs and jars out of the car windows. "We're all right if they don't catch us with the stuff on us," she explained.

This was during Prohibition. We never questioned Granny's actions. She was never wrong. This was true because she said so.

The annex made a connection with the night noises from the back alley and the neighbors' bedroom windows that opened onto it, especially in warm weather.

We were bothered sometimes by drunken arguments and bursts of laughter in the middle of the night or the off-key singing of a tipsy reveler. But what got to us were the pleas of that little boy – the child whose cries I can still hear in my mind almost 90 years later – begging his father to stop beating him.

"Please, Dad, please. I'll be good ... I swear it. Don't hit me again, please, Dad ... please." A whomp of a leather belt hitting a bare backside. A sharp intake of breath – a cross between a sob and a sigh. Punctuated with another whack across raw flesh.

My mother's face, joining mine at the open window, was distorted with pain. She held me to her.

"Why don't we call the police?" I asked during one especially brutal episode.

"They wouldn't come," she said, biting her lip. "A man's home is his castle. It's an old English law that we inherited. We thought it protected us against the king in the old days ... invading our home ... or our castle. We didn't expect ..."

The screams often woke up Mama and me. Papa and Brother slept through it all. Now, in this more enlightened time, the police would come, thank God.

A very special neighbor occupied the northwest corner of Third and East Capitol. It was one of those Capitol Hill surprises – smelly, dusty, dark, genuine gourmet Italian delicatessen, reeking of garlic, Mediterranean spices, and sausages, with olives floating in brine in open casks. But most of all, the air was heavy with the most putrid, foul-smelling cheeses man ever made.

Not intended to appeal to the olfactory sense of a small child. Mama, however, adored the place and every bit of food in it.

I innocently went there with her one hot summer day. The owner had telephoned her, and, in heavily accented, emotional English, lured his favorite customer to come and savor the treats that had just arrived.

As I stood retching in the doorway, Mama and the shopkeeper swooned with ecstasy as they devoured hunks of blue-veined, moldy cheese from which they had just pulled living, writhing worms.

For the next 60 years, the strongest cheese I could handle was Philadelphia cream.

Often, after a funeral that had affected Papa deeply, Mama took him by the hand and led him over to the deli to share her moldy treats. He loved them, too.

She also would try and lift his spirits by urging him to take her to a Mexican restaurant that, I think, was down on Pennsylvania Avenue, S.E.

If my parents' absence had left me feeling abandoned, I'd crawl in bed with them in the middle of the night. But not for long, if they had been to both the Mexican eatery and the Italian deli across the street.

The lingering aroma of over-ripe Gorgonzola mixed with blazing hot chili peppers that permeated the air around them was sure to overcome the scent of embalming fluid that always seemed to hover in our flat.

After a few whiffs, I'd climb back into my own bed, and lie there listening to the mice scurrying near the baseboards. And smelling the hint of embalming fluid. Which I preferred to Gorgonzola.

When I was little, there was a row of brownstone houses across Third Street from us, facing East Capitol. Grant's Row, it was called. This solid block of connected buildings was set well back from the street, and up on a terrace.

I used to think of them as bosomy matrons, wearing Dr. Scholl's sensible shoes that laced, and came in black or brown only.

They were a boring part of the landscape. I barely noticed them. Why bother, when just beyond, in all its glory, was the U.S. Capitol filling our street with beauty and meaning?

At least these brownstones didn't block our view of it.

Despite my negative reaction to them, they must have impressed some people. Based on their architectural gravitas, Grant's Row became in a sense responsible for East Capitol Street's being considered "the most opulent street on Capitol Hill" in the 1920s, according to one critic.

Granny used to say that their peaked roof attics were connected, and that if one caught on fire, they would "all go up in flames."

She also said that there were rats in the long attic passageway. I don't know how she knew that. But nobody ever questioned her when she said such things. And she was usually right.

In 1929 Grant's Row was torn down to make way for the Folger Shakespeare Library – a move that presaged a happy relationship between 301 East Capitol and its new prestigious neighbor.

In 1939 or so, after four generations of Zurhorst funeral directors – with a fifth prospective one waiting in his cradle – the family "gave up the ghost" of the business and moved away.

Ownership of the pre-Civil War building changed hands several times before it met its destiny in the mid-60s when the Folger bought 301 East Capitol and several other buildings in that block.

Because of its historic value and prime location, two blocks from the Capitol, 301 and many of its neighbors were saved from the wrecking ball and given a vibrant new life by the Folger.

The entire interiors of the funeral parlors, apartments and work space were gutted to make room for the Folger's Haskell Center for performance and education programs.

As if caught up in its own *Midsummer Night's Dream*, the funeral parlors turned into a place of magic, where the once silent walls rang with metal glancing off metal as actors and even ordinary people learned the art of swordplay of the Elizabethan era, where school children danced to the rhythms of early music, and the sounds of hautboys, tambourines, recorders, drums and all manner of medieval and Renaissance instruments filled the formerly muted space.

The Haskell Center became home to the noted Folger Consort, which had its first season in 1977, and has since become known throughout the world for its magnificent performances – live and recorded. Much of its life emanated from 301.

For a time, costumes and props for the many Folger productions, Shakespearean and otherwise, found a home at the old parlors. (It now houses business offices connected to the widespread dramatic and cultural center that the Folger has become.)

Costumes heavy with seed pearls and ruffs and farthingales and fake cabuchon jewels filled the once drab rooms with outfits waiting their turn in the spotlight of the stage. And where satin-lined caskets six feet long were once patiently on display, there must have been at least one set of very different caskets – small and made of gold, silver or lead – determining Portia's future in productions yet to come. Did anyone catch the irony of the caskets?

Was there, perhaps, one lone skull tucked away on a ledge somewhere in what had been our living room? Yorick, it would have been. "I knew him, Horatio."

Oh, how my mother would have reveled in this transformation, this rebirth, of 301 East Capitol Street.

It suited her much better than the funeral parlors.

∽

A few years ago, my teenaged California grandson Joshua knocked on the front door of the Folger-owned 301 East Capitol. He asked to look around the building, after explaining the family connection – but not the family business. The Folger people graciously gave him the tour. No questions until the end.

Joshua was waiting with adolescent glee. At last one asked, "Why is this drain in the floor?"

"To drain the embalming fluid," he explained.

He said he wished they had freaked out more.

CHAPTER 4

MOURNING

Even though we lived over the funeral parlors, I had had no personal acquaintance with death as a child until that frightening time of warning in Atlantic City. I was only three or four years old at the first sign.

There's no memory of fear from that time. No memory of the ocean, either, nor of the boardwalk, nor much of anything beyond Mama's screaming for help down the elevator shaft of the hotel.

I do still hear remnants of her appalled reaction during the crisis when Brother told of taking me to breakfast at Childs restaurant on the boardwalk. (I couldn't have been older than three, and Brother eight.)

"You told the waitress to keep the change?!" she sounded panicked. "But, Snooie, I gave you a $20 bill."

I think we had French fries. Just French fries.

Knowing what happened later, I can only guess that Papa had a heart attack while we were staying at a small hotel on the boardwalk – a hotel without telephones in the rooms, or a restaurant with room service, or a doctor. Brother was taking me out to breakfast because Mama couldn't leave Papa.

Eventually, a doctor came. But I don't think my father went to a hospital during the emergency, nor at any time later.

This event happened in the early 1920s. Afterwards, my father seemed to be his usual exuberant, vital self, bestowing wide grins and "little smiles" upon all who came within his amiable circle. But how could I tell? I had known him such a short time.

One morning a few years later, in January 1925, Papa stayed in bed and didn't go downstairs to work. I was playing with my doll house when I heard him say to Mama, "I think I could eat a little something."

I draw a blank on what happened next, except for Mama's weeping, and clinging to the doorway of the bedroom. "He died hungry," she cried over and over. "He died hungry."

I have no recollection of sorrow or sense of loss, just a compulsion to insist on reality as I saw it – a lifelong pattern with me, asserting itself even in those dark moments.

Stop saying that he died hungry, I wanted to say. *It isn't as if we are poor and he starved. He was just asking for a snack.*

Weep because he's gone. But don't weep because he was hungry when he died. That's not the point.

Such thoughts were crowding my head as I followed my mother around the apartment, clinging to her. But saying nothing.

Not my finest hour.

In the accepted practice of the Twenties, my mother went "into mourning" for my father for a year after his death. Immediately after Papa died, Granny and a few of Mama's aunts joined forces to see that she had a choice of somber black dresses, hats, coats, gloves, shoes, hose and veils.

A range of veils varying in thickness covered the dining room table and living room sofa for her selection.

Papa at Cape May, early 1920s.

I hated those veils. They covered my mother's face and cut her off from me.

Since I had never experienced death in my immediate family, I didn't know the rules. Would Mama wear a thick, black veil for the rest of her life?

Would she cry forever?

Where had Papa gone?

Would he ever come back?

What was going to happen to Brother and me now?

If I discussed any of these mysteries with anyone, I don't recall such talks. I just went on playing in my doll house and humming to myself.

Mostly, I hummed the tune to "Ioway, Ioway, That's Where the Tall Corn Grows." That song had made a direct hit on my senses the summer before, when I was five.

I first heard it when Granny and Mama and Brother and I went to the Shriners' Parade that we watched from bleachers on Pennsylvania Avenue, N.W. As a 32nd Degree Mason, and a Shriner, Papa was to march in the parade, exotic costume, fez and all.

It was well past my bedtime when Papa's group reached us. Asleep on Mama's lap, I was awakened to the bizarre sight of my father garbed in some Arabian Nights outfit, waving wildly to us, with a big smile on his face and the tassel of his fez swinging in a wide arc, as he marched down the Avenue.

For some mysterious reason, I burst into terrified screams that drew unwelcome attention from the next marching band and several other Masonic delegations that passed us. Then a huge contingent from Iowa appeared before us, singing even louder than I was howling.

"Ioway, Ioway," they sang, "that's where the tall corn grows." I joined in and sang it as the rest of the parade passed by, no matter what they were singing or playing. I sang it on the streetcar on the way home, and apparently in every waking moment thereafter, until my father could take it no longer.

"Ioway, Ioway, that's where the tall corn grows."

"Ioway, Ioway, that's where the tall corn grows."

"Ioway, Ioway ..."

"Sissy ... sweetheart ... please," he begged. "Could you *not* sing that song for just a *little* while? Please?"

I would stop, then, without thinking, drift into it again. "Ioway, Ioway, that's where the tall ...." Sometimes I'd just hum the tune.

Papa began giving me pennies to stop the music.

Brother, of course, wanted to get into the act. He asked for his own blackmail pennies for not singing at all.

I don't know what perverse scheme drove me to resume humming the tune again after Papa's funeral, a few years after the parade and its follow-up. I did it unconsciously.

And I didn't notice that whenever I started humming "Ioway, Ioway ..." Mama would quietly sob. It was Granny who stopped me. "Can't you see that that song makes your mother sad?" she asked me.

I couldn't see it. In fact, I didn't even know I was humming.

All these years later, that inane music still surfaces in my consciousness from time to time. But I don't sing it or even hum it any more.

It was a relief to learn that the heavy, almost opaque veil was just for the funeral. Not that I went to the funeral, but I saw her come home, wearing it. She replaced it with lighter-weight veils as the months passed. But for an eternity to a little girl, she wore solid black.

A year after Papa's death, when Mama added a touch of purple to her wardrobe, it was as if the sun had risen after an unending night.

Was it a purple ribbon on a black hat? Or a purple hat? I'm not sure. It was something purple that lightened the darkness. Of that I'm sure. It was very welcome.

After that time, color gradually reappeared in Mama's clothes.

Although I certainly don't advocate a return to the custom of "deep mourning," my mother's unremitting acknowledgment that something truly terrible had happened was inescapable and unforgettable. The death of my father was not taken lightly. He was 44 years old. She was 32.

CHAPTER 5

CAPITOL HILL'S GRAND DESIGN

As Oscie and I roamed the streets of Capitol Hill, we were much too close to the details to see the Grand Design. Why did I skip on Pennsylvania Avenue, S.E., and walk quietly down East Capitol Street when we went to Lincoln Park?

Without words to shape the thought, I felt, somehow, the distinctive tempo, the identifying rhythm of the streets and avenues of this neighborhood, which hadn't grown organically, as most neighborhoods grow. Capitol Hill is the incarnation of a concept as radical in its way as self-government. It is a planned community.

I was not aware of just how carefully planned it was until in writing this book, I discovered *Grand Avenues* by Scott W. Berg, published in 2007 by Pantheon Books. Subtitled "The Story of the French Visionary Who Designed Washington, D.C.," the book reintroduced me to Capitol Hill, an entire lifetime after our warm friendship had begun. Before reading it, I merely knew what it was like to live there. Now I know *why* it was like it was and still is.

It's no accident – or lack of urban planning – that there are scattered throughout Capitol Hill corner grocery stores, a bank a block or two away, a barbershop next to a four-story, bay-windowed mansion. Such mixed use of land grew out of Pierre (he preferred the Americanized Peter) L'Enfant's Grand Design for the city of Washington, District of Columbia. It's a democratic concept, reflecting the system of government, as Berg so clearly describes it.

Nowhere in this diamond-shaped piece of land, carved out of Maryland and at one time a sliver of Virginia, is L'Enfant's vision more realized than on Capitol Hill, where Congress's House stands, and in the Capitol Hill neighborhood, where people live.

L'Enfant thought big and he thought long range. This 100-square-mile territory he was dealing with was mostly empty as he rode over it, filled with low-lying swamps and scattered farms, slave quarters and outbuildings.

He saw it as a New World City.

Sophisticates in London, Paris, Madrid, and other large cities of Europe laughed at the arrogance of the L'Enfant plan. A 100-square-mile city would be bigger than any other city in the world. Who did he think would inhabit such a vast space? And one located on an undistinguished site whose only excuse for being there was that it was geographically midway between northern Maine and southern Georgia.

That was George Washington's idea.

L'Enfant's idea for filling this diamond was to begin with squares and circles forming small town centers that would gradually grow into larger towns until they melded, and, eventually, filled out into a city. Each population center had its own necessities and conveniences, hence the corner grocery stores and other amenities that remain.

According to *Grand Avenues*, he envisioned different kinds of neighborhoods blending as time went on. So there are homey little streets in neat alphabetical order crossing equally narrow streets in numerical order on a neat grid. Slicing diagonally through these unpretentious precincts are broad, leafy boulevards that boast a bit more up-scale housing, set back from the avenues by long lawns which give the effect of even broader thoroughfares traversing the neighborhood, as Berg shows us.

There is a rich architectural mix in all of Capitol Hill, with many of the houses gladly sharing a wall or two with the next-door neighbor. A four-story Victorian red brick with bay window top to bottom may well find itself up against a cozy, two-story clapboard from Federal times.

This, then, is Capitol Hill – home to the Eastern Market, the Marine Barracks, Congressional Cemetery (outside the boundaries of the Historic District, but a Capitol Hill institution nonetheless), the Navy Yard (off The Hill at the Anacostia River, though of The Hill and its people), Folger Library, Library of Congress, Supreme Court, and lately – relatively speaking – Metro, Starbucks, and restricted parking.

All of this grand neighborhood takes its identity and its location from its relation to the Capitol of the United States. That is the hub of the entire city. Everything within the boundaries of the District of Columbia has an address with S.E., N.E., S.W., or N.W. attached, depending on its orientation to the Capitol.

And throughout Capitol Hill, just up the street, or behind the trees, or over the rooftops is always that Great White Presence, the Capitol of the United States of America.

Match that, Beacon Hill, Nob Hill, Pocantico Hills, Shaker Heights, Pelham Manor, Grosse Pointe, Palm Beach, Palm Springs. Match it if you can.

CHAPTER 6

GETTYSBURG

The weather was damp and cold on November 18, 1863, when a disparate group gathered at the old train station at the foot of Capitol Hill. A number of dignitaries, both foreign and domestic, together with security guards, had already boarded the special train when the President's carriage drove up.

Mr. Lincoln was not feeling well. He had a cold and a slight fever. Calling in sick was not an option.

He had been asked to offer a "few appropriate remarks" at the dedication of a new Union cemetery at Gettysburg, and this special train was to take him and a select group of passengers there.

Mr. Lincoln was painfully aware that the featured speaker was Edward Everett, a man of awesome talent, known nationwide as an orator. Mr. Lincoln didn't see himself as a match for such as Edward Everett.

The President had written a few words already, at the White House, and had tucked them in his coat pocket, to be added to later. What would be "appropriate remarks" in his awkward position, he wondered.

He had been sitting for a while in the car reserved for members of the Cabinet, various officials, and top-ranking military officers, when he heard that the men of the United States Marine Band – "The President's Own" – were traveling with him on the train. All 27 of them. Including Antonio Sousa, John Philip Sousa's father, and August Schroeder, my great-grandfather. Both were also in the Marine Band when it played for Mr. Lincoln's first inaugural ceremonies in 1861.

When he could politely leave the "Big Wigs" and their endless political chatter, Mr. Lincoln slipped away to be with his men in the rear car.

"He came and joined us," wrote Second Lieutenant Henry Clay Cochrane, an officer assigned to the Marine Barracks, in a letter to his parents. The Marine quoted the President as saying, when he took a seat among them, "'Ha! This is much better.'" And there he stayed until they arrived in Gettysburg a few hours later.

The dedication ceremonies were to be held the next day, November 19. It was another bone-chilling, dreary morning. Mr. Lincoln's cold and fever were worse. At least he had finished writing his brief "appropriate remarks."

In the wet procession to the cemetery, the President was given a horse much too small for him, and his long arms and legs dangled ludicrously, making his six-foot four frame appear more ungainly than usual.

After an interminable opening prayer, the Marine Band played a hymn. It was followed by a two-hour impassioned oration by Edward Everett. The drizzling rain never ceased. An additional band performed.

Finally, President Lincoln was introduced to the cold and wet crowd, who by now must have wanted nothing more than to go home.

He delivered his brief speech – destined to be enshrined forever in stone and in the heart of the people as "The Gettysburg Address" – and took his seat to a smattering of applause. It was over before the photographer assigned to record the historic moment on film could take even one picture. Actually, he was mainly concerned that he didn't have a picture that his editor could run in tomorrow's newspaper.

Deeply disappointed in his own performance, and embarrassed, Mr. Lincoln told a friend, "That speech won't scour." He shook his head. "It's a flat failure."

The correspondent for the *London Times* reported: "The ceremony was rendered ludicrous by the sallies of that poor President Lincoln .... Anyone more dull and commonplace it would not be easy to produce."

On the train trip back to Washington, Mr. Lincoln sat alone, a damp cloth on his forehead.

CHAPTER 7

LIFE AT 318 A

Before I was old enough to go to school, there was a certain rhythm in our lives that corresponded to the schedule of Congress: adjourn for the summer, convene in the fall. We both were seeking relief from Washington's heat and humidity.

While the Congress returned to home states, we Zurhorsts went around the corner to Granny's – my mother's mother – at 318 A Street, S.E., to escape the heat.

Granny's existed before there were retirement communities, assisted living facilities, or nursing homes, shelters for abused families, tough love programs for wayward children – or just summer getaways. The house was a Mecca for those in any kind of need.

Granny was a cross between Mother Teresa and Queen Victoria. Generous, imperious, charitable – all these, and, without question, the CEO of both her family and her in-laws' families. She could have coined the statement, "I'm in charge here." Instead, she frequently affirmed, without fear of contradiction, "I've never been wrong in my life." Yet, I don't know what any one of us who benefited by her largesse would have done without her.

Follow the trail that Mr. and Mrs. John Schroeder (Granny and Grandpap) left through Capitol Hill via the Census and city directories, and find that throughout their long married life there was always a great-aunt, a brother, several sisters, mothers-in-law, and/ or assorted ladies in distress in residence. Indeed, a great many households of the late 1800s and early 1900s included someone outside the immediate family. These extra inhabitants went beyond grandparents in three-generation homes; some were boarders, some distant relatives, and, in the more affluent households, there were live-in servants, identified as maids, coachmen, stable boys, etc. Statistics indicating educational levels showed that most of the latter group had no schooling at all.

In Granny's house (never called Grandpap's house) on A Street, in addition to Granny and Grandpap, and occasionally three or all four of us Zurhorsts, there lived at one time or another, Aunt Ellie Whitney, Aunt Ellie Sanderson (before my time, but their names sound like Granny's English side of the family); Granny's sisters, Aunt Addie, Aunt Gertie, and Aunt Katie; Aunt Emma (no relation, but she had been a "ward" of Granny's parents, who also took in several Portuguese sailors who jumped ship to live in the U.S.); distant relatives Aunt Arabella, Aunt Mamie and Shelton (a grandmother, mother, and grown son who showed up at unexpected times); and Grandma Zurhorst, my father's mother. Plus the occasional out-of-control teen in need of a stern hand – Granny's.

Of course, they didn't all live there at the same time, but it was a remarkably expansive house, despite having just four bedrooms and one bath. Nobody was ever turned away. Nobody went hungry.

Most were ladies who had never married or who had been married and abandoned or widowed or abused by drunken husbands. There was one distant cousin in her 40s who used to show up covered in bruises, with one or both eyes swollen shut, two blond little boys clinging to her skirts and cowering down into their belted jackets. They would stay for a few days until the mother announced that she thought it would be "safe to go home now."

Granny's house, 318 A Street, S.E. (present day).

Granny and her ubiquitous fly swatter, with me at Cape May.

Granny reserved special loathing for this cousin's husband. With him, it wasn't "the drink" that could be blamed. He was what Granny called "a sober devil." That was the worst kind.

Cousin Shelton, Aunt Arabella's grandson, had some strikes against him, according to Granny's sister Gertie, who doted on him. First, his father had been a drunkard. Second, he hadn't had a chance to get a good education. And third, he reputedly had been hit on the head by a coal scuttle as a child. Or those were Aunt Gertie's explanations for his behavior. Shelton was somewhere in his 20s when he and his grandmother and mother would seek refuge at Granny's. He was tall, well-built, and looked somewhat like Tom Mix, the John Wayne cowboy of the Twenties. He worked only when the job required a uniform. He loved to dress up. Each job lasted only a few months.

One night when I was a very young child and staying at Granny's without the rest of my immediate family, I was awakened in the middle of the night by the front door slamming, followed by a shouted, "I'll knock his goddamn block off. That's what I'll do." It was Shelton. The smell of his Lucky Strike cigarette drifted upstairs.

As he made his way up the steps, I could hear others stirring in rooms along the hall, but there were no lights on yet. I got up and went looking for Granny. Where was she? Everything would be all right if I could just find Granny.

Then somebody pulled the cord on the dimmer light in the hallway – a bare light bulb that had a chain on it that made it shine from very dim to bright, gradually.

When it came on, there was Shelton, right in front of me at the bathroom door. He went in. I could see him in the half light, relieving himself. I had never before seen a man do this. I stared, transfixed.

He flipped his lit cigarette into the unflushed toilet. It made a little hissing sound.

I was peering into the foul bowl when Granny arrived. "Now see what you've done," she said to Shelton as he staggered away from her. "You've awakened this child, along with the rest of the house."

He just walked away, cursing under his breath, and lighting another Lucky Strike. Granny took me into her bed with her. I went right back to sleep – but not before hearing Aunt Gertie's troubled voice from the hall crying, "Poor boy. He can't help it."

To feed all those under Granny's roof required prodigious amounts of food. And work. And money. They were not a wealthy couple – Granny and Grandpap – by any means. In fact, Grandpap held down two jobs, one in a bank by day and the second as an orchestra conductor, probably to support Granny's in-home charities. And her chosen lifestyle didn't come cheap. Her strongest insult was to say something or someone was cheap.

As opposed to the steaks and chops and tiny squabs we ate around the corner at 301 East Capitol, Granny's large household dined on beef stews, seafood chowders, chicken pot pies (the lighter-than-air, many-layered crust made extra delicious by pure lard or bacon fat) and chicken fricassees with big dumplings. No twenty-first century chicken dish comes close to that chicken fricassee, starting with tremendous, old hens with a chicken flavor unrelated to the skinless, boneless, tasteless unchicken of today. After simmering for hours in rich broth, enhanced by "the best butter" and pure thick cream made even thicker by an egg yolk mixture, the result was ambrosia, a treat for the most cultivated of palates. Or the most clogged of arteries.

Except for the pot pies that were topped by a crust, these easily stretched main dishes were served in an extra large ironstone tureen with a big ladle. Placed in the middle of the dining room table, the tureen stood directly under an inverted, flowered glass dome of a lampshade that hung low over the table. Glass-beaded fringe dangled from the rim.

Just before dinner one evening, Brother and I were the first at the table. The filled tureen was in place, the lid still on. I was kneeling on a dining room chair and, for lack of anything better to do, began playing with the fringe on the lamp. The little beads felt greasy to the touch. Then there was a "ping," as one came down and hit the closed tureen. I plucked it off and tucked it in my pocket.

The incident triggered Brother's endless capacity for mischief. Instantly, he leaned over, removed the lid and started milking the beads off of the fringe and into the stew.

I was appalled. "I'm gonna tell Granny," I said.

He just laughed and said he'd say I did it.

As the ladies began gathering around the table, Brother took his place in silence, the cowlick at the crown of his head standing up stiffer than usual, like a signal of danger.

Nobody seemed to notice. And nobody choked on a bead or cracked a tooth, either. Brother and I kept looking around the table, waiting for some excitement – a cry of outrage or a gasp from a blocked air passage. But nothing happened. It was a great disappointment.

After an uneventful meal, Brother's "special cocktail" was more potent than usual that night. I could never understand how he was allowed to get away with it, but often when we were at Granny's, he would mix up a noxious drink and bully one of the old ladies to down it. The diabolic mixture consisted of whatever liquids he could find at the table – leftovers of cold coffee, dregs of tea leaves, a spot of cream, a splash of salad oil tempered by a drop of vinegar from the cruets always on the table, and maybe some fresh peach juice from the bottom of a dessert bowl. Aunt Emma – no relation – was one of his favorite victims, although nobody's favorite person. The only time she related to us or the rest of the residents was at Christmas, when she offered stuffed dates she had filled herself – with dust and lint from under her bed, Brother said. That's where she kept them.

Whoever he chose to drink his evil brew would whine and complain and draw back in disgust as he thrust the cup on her. Eventually, the chosen "aunt" would take a few sips just to shut him up.

He didn't dare do this when Granny was in the room.

Many of these women had not worked outside the home. Most had a limited education. Granny had been graduated from business school, so she was ahead of the pack. And she had a full life, running her extended family.

Two of her sisters – Gertie and Addie – worked as bookkeepers at Congressional Cemetery. They were completely opposite types.

Aunt Gertie was small, lively, emotional, and easily excited. So Brother liked to scare her with mechanical mice or tales of ghosts rising up out of caskets, which he made up on the spot. She had been engaged to my grandfather's brother Frank, who died of TB before they were to have married. He was very young. In line with the emotional climate of the times, she considered the very handsome Frank Schroeder to be the one true love of her life. When he died, she felt there could not be any other man for her, and her life was over.

She hadn't reckoned on the role Shelton was to play in her emotions. For good or ill, he provided the outlet she needed for her unspent store of tender, loving care.

Aunt Addie was the intellectual of the family. Rather stout, with a swarthy complexion, she was forever quoting Shakespeare – words that had an alien sound in this setting.

One hot day, after the long walk back from Congressional Cemetery, I was there when she came in, flushed and damp. She went straight upstairs to the room she shared with Aunt Gertie. Apparently she left the door open, because I could hear a plop – something soft but heavy hitting the floor. Her whalebone corset, I knew. The only one I had ever seen. Formidable!

"Oh, that this too, too solid flesh would melt," she cried. "Thaw, resolve itself into a dew." When she came down for dinner, her body shape had changed radically – sort of like a once sharply defined cold stick of butter that had been left out in the sun too long, and was, indeed, melting.

Aunt Katie was the gentle one, the one who did the dishes and never complained. "Kate," we called her. She didn't go out at all, just sat at the dining room table most of the day and read the newspaper. I used to wonder if she really was reading it. She was "a little slow," Granny said.

⌘

Occasionally, a few of the "aunts" gathered in the front parlor in the evening. Generally, they speculated on who would "go" during the next winter. "I think it's Raymond's turn," said one of them (they blur in my memory). "No," offered another, "I think Raymond has a few years left. More like Ellie's time. You know she has that female complaint that the doctors couldn't treat. Poor thing."

They spared their housemates in this game of "Next" and concentrated on members of the extended family who weren't present.

In the hall near the front door at Granny's was a large hat rack with a mirror, several hooks for hats, and a hinged seat that lifted to reveal heaps of overshoes – used only for going to funerals. "Gravesites can be soggy," one of the aunts explained one day before leaving for the cemetery in one of Papa's funeral limousines.

Each evening, they turned on the Atwater Kent radio in the front parlor and listened to The Cliquot Club Eskimos playing the tunes of the era. If the weather was bad, static ruined the reception. So the favorite source of pleasure was the wind-up phonograph, with records of John McCormack, or Caruso and Galli-Curci and Rosa Ponselle. There was a kind of minstrel act on records, too. I remember one joke from the show: "This says take one pill three times a day .... You can't do that." I thought that was very funny.

Despite the surprisingly cheerful, red-flocked wallpaper in the front hall of Granny's house, a wisp of doom seemed to hover over the aunts who gathered in the parlor every night after dinner.

They sat there, eyes on the Gothic-shaped, Atwater-Kent radio, in dead silence. Then, at the appointed hour – was it 7 p.m.? – here it came: "Yoo-hoo, Missus Bloo-om. Is annabody? ... You was expecting mebbe Missus Nussbaum?"

Smiles all around the parlor. Heads nodding in welcome to an old friend, Molly Goldberg, bless her. The gloom lifted, wafted off on a cloud of overcooked cabbage, and all was well with the world.

They listened to Amos and Andy, too, around dinnertime. "That rascal!" Aunt Emma would scold the blowhard Andy, on the nightly visit that the household waited for all day.

Other aunts would commiserate with "poor Amos, he tries so hard to make Andy behave." They were very real to these ladies, who had a special fondness for the sensible, honest, Amos.

Apart from all the rest of the household was the reclusive Grandma Zurhorst, nee Emma Wilk McGowan, quietly keeping to herself, except for meals. She was my father's mother.

Even though I wasn't yet four when she died, I remember her clearly – and very fondly. She was the only member of the family who played games with me. She would rather formally invite me into her room, then sit me down beside a large steamer trunk, which, when she opened it, smelled of lavender. (She told me it was the trunk her family had brought over from Scotland when they came to America. It is now in my basement, no longer smelling of lavender, but redolent with memories.)

From it, she took out a Parcheesi board, and she taught me to play the game. We spoke very little. I remember her as a delicate, vulnerable little lady with soft, white hair and a soft, gentle voice.

Grandma Zurhorst was different from the others at Granny's. She didn't belong to the clan that Granny and Mama and the "aunts" belonged to, and the difference showed.

I didn't feel a part of that clan, either. Sometimes when I fell silent, or spoke very softly, Granny or Mama would call me "Grandma Zurhorst." I knew it wasn't meant as a compliment.

I used to wonder why she was living at Granny's. Why didn't she have her own house? What happened to Grandfather Zurhorst? I wouldn't know the answer to those questions until I was a grown woman with almost-grown children of my own.

And until the mystery of 203 Third Street was solved.

CHAPTER 8

STREET THEATER IN OUR NEIGHBORHOOD

Watching the floodlights come on at twilight to illuminate the Capitol Dome was a winter ritual from our windows at 301 East Capitol. The summer ritual on A Street – at Granny's – was waiting for the lamplighter each evening at sunset, as he made his way up the street, lighting the gas lamps one by one. They gave off a faint, golden glow that seemed to deepen the shadows.

When he reached St. Mark's Church, where A Street deadends at Third, he turned the corner toward Pennsylvania Avenue, his ladder on his shoulder, and walked out of view.

The second part of this street show followed in a few minutes, and always filled me with a delicious, spine-tingling fear, as I stood on Granny's porch, waiting.

Pretty soon it would start – that ghostly call from out of the darkness.

"Who da?" The voice was male, rich baritone, African.

A moment of silence. Then, "Who da say who da?"

From the sound, you could tell that he was turning his head as he questioned the empty street, in search of ... what?

He drew closer. With every few steps he added to the cry. "Who da say who da when I say who da?" And next, "Who da say who da when I say who da say who da?" When the accumulated "who das" became too cumbersome to handle, "Who da" would stop, look all around him, and then start all over again.

"Who da" was harmless, Granny insisted, and she was right, of course. Harmless, but scary.

The cast of characters on East Capitol tended to be more sophisticated than those on A Street.

The organ grinder and his perky little monkey were the delight of everybody on the street. Dressed in a bellhop's uniform, the tiny fellow hopped onto anybody's arm, if welcome. I never saw him surprise or frighten anyone by an unwanted leap. He seemed to enjoy the show more than the audience that dropped coins into his tin cup.

His Italian master smiled and inclined his head in thanks to every giver. And throughout the show, he was grinding out "Come Back to Sorrento," or something close, on his hand organ.

Another animal visitor that we waited for was the man with the pony. The cry went up from way down East Capitol Street, "The pony's here," and children came out of the houses to have their pictures taken on the pony. I don't think we ever got a ride, not even in a small circle.

But we got a picture, and I wonder how many turn up today on black album pages, held by little triangles.

East Capitol Street's version of the mysterious "Who da" on A Street was a willowy, ethereal creature who appeared on pleasant, temperate evenings, strolling on East Capitol Street. She was elegantly clad in pastels from head to toe and beyond. Her costume was finished off with a matching parasol, which she twirled languidly, ever so seductively from time to time. Each outfit was perfectly dyed – she couldn't have bought it off the rack – so that everything matched. She had a powder blue one, a lavender one, a pink one, a peach one, and a yellow one – shoes, hose, dress, gloves, hat and parasol all the exact same hue.

We all watched for her – sometimes from the office downstairs, where one of the men who worked for the business would usually be the first to spot her. She paraded always on the north side of the street. "Here she comes," Fred or Lee would call out, and the rest of us leaped to the window. The men made bets on which color she would wear that day.

It's strange that we referred to her as "The Lavender Lady," since her wardrobe just about ran the gamut of the pastel spectrum. To the end, none of us ever saw her enter or leave a building. She just appeared, passed by, and disappeared up the street.

These neighborhood characters have become extinct, replaced by Seinfeld and Google and DVDs and chat rooms and iPods and other twenty-first century entertainment.

As a child, I saw them as two-dimensional beings, appearing, as on a stage, for our entertainment, then exeunt, downstage right, out of our lives.

A Street vendors were Tom the huckster and his horse Daisy, wearing a straw hat, with her ears protruding. Tom sold vegetables and came year-round, hawking his wares.

Another cast of characters sold summer fruit. The man who brought the season's first strawberries had a distinctive call – "Straaaaaaaawberries," long drawn out, with a playful rising inflection at the end. He sang it.

"Sissie" on the pony that went nowhere.

The sound for watermelons came from deep in the throat – "Woedamelon, woedamelon/fresh off da vine/woedamelon, woedamelon/red to the rind."

It was an exciting time when first fruits of the harvest came into season. Women ran out of the houses from all over the neighborhood to get the treats. Strawberries were never bigger than a quarter, were sweet as honey, and dripped juice. New corn and tomatoes thrilled us all.

There were other voices from the street, like the iceman who announced himself simply, as "Iceman." He, too, had a horse-drawn wagon. At Granny's house, Aunt Gertie was responsible for putting a flat cardboard square in the front window, indicating the number of desired pounds of ice. Aunt Gertie sometimes forgot. Granny would chew her out, listing the foods that would be ruined by tomorrow without ice.

The iceman, with powerful shoulders, would heft a block of 20, 30, 40, 50 pounds onto his back with huge tongs. He wore a thick leather garment between his skin and the ice. I would watch this show of strength with awe.

The man who came to tend the furnace or take out the ashes from the coal furnace arrived silently, just walked in through the always unlocked door. There must have been somebody else bringing in fresh coal every week or whenever, but he failed to survive in my memory. I do know this: Granny's house was distinguished by having a basement. Not everyone on the street did.

The ragman was vocal, and announced his arrival as he pushed a small wooden cart. No horse. He would come out of the alley between A and B Streets, S.E. (B Street is now Independence Avenue.)

That's where the washerwoman emerged from, too. She came pushing an old baby carriage with a crooked wheel that squeaked. The carriage was piled high with sun-bleached, sweet-smelling white linens, ironed and neatly folded. She dropped them off at Granny's, and picked up the soiled batch to take away.

I wonder how much she was paid to hand-wash, hang dry, and iron these mounds of linens from Granny's crowded household. And where were they going, the ragman, the ashman, the washerwoman, and others without faces or names who did our dirty work and then disappeared up the alley and out of our world? I never thought to ask – or even wonder.

And then one day I entered their world, briefly. Mama and I were "paying a call" on our much-loved Louise Ford, who had been "in the family," although not of it, since before my mother was born. My mother had brought Lou some clothes she didn't wear any more. They both had trim figures and wore the same size.

Lou lived "down there," in back of the first House Office Building, the Cannon (named for the crude old tyrant from Texas, "Uncle" Joe Cannon, who was Speaker of the House of Representatives from 1903 to 1911 and a Member of the House for 46 years).

Every few years, newspapers ran exposés of these dwellings, referred to as the "slums in the shadow of the Capitol."

Granny always dismissed the subject with a remark about the sun's having to rise in the northeast or set in the northwest to cast the Capitol's shadow on those houses. Subject closed.

Capitol Hill old-timers – or cave dwellers – are more aware than most people of the points of the compass, because of their relation to the Capitol, from which all D.C. addresses get their bearings.

Lou's home was an ancient, tree-shaded, mossy brick, sagging a bit but not dilapidated. The front yard, like most on that street, was enclosed by an iron fence, rusting and missing its gate.

I loved to go there, especially when Lou let me play with an old, upright wooden organ powered by bellows, a cast-off from her church. The tiny rooms were packed with cast-offs – furniture from both my grandparents' homes. There was a lovely but threadbare rosewood sofa from Granny's A Street house, an oak side-board from my grandfather's childhood home on Ninth Street, S.E., and unmatched china from both houses – all discarded but not thrown away. Their "heirlooms" were too loaded with family memories to be trash. So they were thrust upon Lou.

She always accepted the gifts with grace, as if she were getting the very thing she had wanted all of her life. She must have wondered where she would put it all.

Beyond Lou's house, down a slight hill, the neighborhood grew poorer, with more dirt than grass in the yards and rubble leaning against the houses.

In one cluttered yard, a familiar object caught my eye – the washerwoman's crooked-wheel baby carriage. The same one she rolled out of the alley every Monday, bringing Granny's clean linens to 318 A.

I stared at it as Mama went in the house with Lou. So, I thought, when the washerwoman disappeared up the alley, she didn't just cease to be, she was on her way home. Here. Down the street from Lou's. She had a home, a life, maybe even a family. Slowly, she was becoming a human being to me.

As I stood grappling with this disturbing reality, Mama and Lou came out, looking for me.

"What are you doing out here?" Mama asked.

'Nothing," I said.

"What are you staring at?"

"I bet I know," said Lou, giving me a hug. "You recognize Phyllis's baby carriage, don't you, precious?"

"Who's Phyllis?" my mother frowned.

"Don't you know Phyllis? She's the laundress who does Miss Odie's linens. A *fine* woman. Got two *fine* children." Lou shook her head in sadness. "Lost her husband a few years ago. Killed by a runaway horse. *Fine* man. Good father."

On the silent walk back home, I was trying to sort out my feelings, to grasp the strange facts I had learned. The washerwoman who ceased to exist for me when I could no longer see her – or no longer hear the crooked wheel of the baby carriage wobble on the cobblestones – had a real house and a name, even had children, just like Granny and Mama and Aunt Susan and Uncle Clarence. She had once had a husband. And she wasn't a washerwoman. She was a laundress. A real person.

I hadn't thought beyond the alley.

"You're very quiet," said Mama, when we got to Third Street. "What are you thinking about, Grandma Zurhorst?"

"Nothing," I said, staring straight ahead.

CHAPTER 9

LOU AND JEFF

Lou Ford and Jeff (unrelated to each other) had been "in the family" for generations, though neither was a blood relative. (I can hear Jeff howling with laughter at the thought of being an actual member of a family headed by Granny. He'd probably say that he would try to get himself adopted out.) I think both had originally worked from a young age for my great-grandfather Schroeder's family at 524 Ninth Street, S.E.

Lou also could have been a sort of nanny to my mother. She used to tell me how beautiful my mother had been as a child and throughout her life and how she would take my teenage mother on walks past the Marine Barracks. "She'd step out like a proud horse." Lou's soft brown eyes opened wide at the memory. "Shiny black hair she had, caught up in a big white bow. Those men at the barracks, they'd look sweet at her, and I'd say, 'Just keep walking, baby, and keep your eyes straight ahead.' They couldn't help gazing at her. Wasn't their fault. They were men."

Small-boned and light-skinned with a tiny, graceful figure, Lou had a smile as comforting when she was in her eighties as it was when I first knew her. She was about my grandmother's age, and the only person I knew whom Granny treated as an equal. In fact, Lou was Granny's best and only close friend.

Jeff, on the other hand, was more a "worthy opponent" to my grandmother. A large ebony-skinned man, he had worked as a handyman within the family since he was a child. He also had done odd jobs at the Marine Barracks. Just before the war with Spain, in 1898, Jeff enlisted in the U.S. Army, and according to him, rode horseback up San Juan Hill right next to Teddy Roosevelt. "If you see a picture of us riding up that hill, look for the one with his hat on backwards. That's me," he told us hundreds of times. "Look for the one with his hat on backwards." Jeff often repeated himself just to be sure you had heard him the first time. It was hard to miss his point because he also shouted.

Granny had a soft voice, but, as the matriarch of the combined Shelton, Schroeder and Zurhorst families, she spoke with unquestioned authority. No one dared argue with Granny except Jeff.

"Jeff, come back here. Look at the corner behind the sofa. You call that clean?" she'd call out to Jeff as he was house-cleaning.

"Now, Miss Odie," he'd wail, "there you go again. How'm I gonna get this job done if you keep makin' me do every little thing over?"

"Well, do it right the first time," she'd say and they would have at it through every room of the house. Jeff said many, many times, "I been a good soldier, rode up San Juan Hill right beside Teddy Roosevelt, never had a bad mark against me, honorable discharge, but if there was another war, and they let women serve, and Miss Odie was my sergeant, I'd desert. That's the God's truth. I'd desert."

"I heard you the first time," Granny would invariably answer. "Come back here and get to work."

Jeff used to come around to the parlors at 301 and wash the windows of our third-floor apartment, a couple of times a year. He would sit in the windowsill, facing in, and, with a huge pail of water nearby, scrub the windows. When the water got dirty, he would simply toss it to the paved area beneath. He never looked to see if anyone was passing at the moment. He would, however, always yell, "LOOK OUT BELOW!!" At least once, he doused an outraged neighbor who was making a shortcut close to the building.

Jeff did odd jobs at all the family households, wrapped, summer and winter like a mummy, in thick woolen scarves. "What keeps out the cold, keeps out the heat," he claimed, sweat pouring through the wool layers.

What he did best, however, was to sing duets with my mother, who was musically lonely. Jeff claimed to sing "tenor-bass." Actually, he had a deeply resonant, Paul Robeson kind of bass voice that blended perfectly with my mother's dramatic soprano.

Mama so loved to sing with Jeff that she would entice him away from his chores by playing such masculine offerings as, "They're Hangin' Danny Deaver in the Morning'" and "On the Road to Mandalay." He'd start grinning, then looking for Granny, as he edged away from the mop toward the piano, tentatively starting the lyrics.

Gradually, the luscious duets would start, full of lyrical melody and a blending of voices that was as smooth as spun silk.

"There's a Long, Long Trail A-winding Into the Land of My Dreams," they sang, with a tender, gentle beauty, then the gossamer "Whispering Hope," and my special favorite, "Oh, That We Two Were Maying."

I have no idea what Maying means, and I doubt that Jeff knew either – or maybe not even Mama. It didn't matter. And it was a strange wish for this odd couple to be singing their hearts out for. But, by God, they made heavenly music together.

I very much wanted Lou Ford to come to my graduation from Gunston Hall High School, but she was hesitant. She knew that Gunston held to many of the old social mores, and Lou didn't know if she would be welcome there. "We'll see," she said, "Don't worry your head about it child. I'll think of something."

As I stood on that stage with my classmates, I looked over the audience and saw among them, Granny, Brother and his wife, Esther May, but no Lou.

Then, squinting my eyes into thin slits, I could see a little white blob in the last seat on the aisle in the far back of the hall. Just the tilt of it looked familiar. The way Lou held her head …

I ran to that spot as soon as the ceremonies were over. And there was Lou. A Lou I had never seen before – dressed in a crisply starched uniform fit for a proper ladies' maid in an antiquated southern household. The white blob I had spotted from the stage was a tiny, beribboned cap.

Two or three other women of color, in similar uniforms, were seated in the same back row as Lou. They had come to see their "babies" graduate. And they knew their "place." Like actors in a period drama.

That graduation at Gunston was in 1936. The Dark Ages, relatively speaking. Or the beginning of the end of them.

CHAPTER 10

CAPITOL HILL NEIGHBORS

Capitol Hill wasn't very child-friendly in the Twenties. If there were children in our neighborhood, I didn't know them – except for the Puglisi boys next door to us on Third Street. But they were older even than Brother, and he was born five years before I was. Their favorite game was rolling metal trash cans down the tin roof of the lean-to attached to the back of the shop.

Nice kids. Their father was a barber, and we all went to him for haircuts. Well, not Mama. She had long hair that she wore coiled low at the back of her neck.

It wasn't just that there were not other children around; all of Capitol Hill seemed to be becoming decrepit. If Mama weren't having Grandpap's elderly sisters to Sunday dinner, she was making "courtesy calls" on maiden ladies in black dresses who cherished "papa's" memory, and feared that their inheritance was not enough to see them through.

Consequently, their inherited family homes badly needed upkeep and repairs, but the money wasn't there to do it. Many once-elegant houses were falling apart. Capitol Hill was beginning its downhill slide, which didn't begin to reverse upward for the next 30 or more years.

An exception to this aging population was the Tappan family, who lived across the street from Granny on A Street. The Tappans were such a wholesome, normal family that they made me wonder what was wrong with us.

Mrs. Tappan was a slender little woman straight from Ireland. Mr. Tappan was portly, and English. They had five children – Bill, Stella, Rob, Margaret and Nora, ranging in age from 25 to 10 when I first knew them. But, best of all, they had Unkie living with them. I wished we had Unkie living with us.

He was everything the great-aunts living at Granny's were not – he was relatively young, thin as a rail, funny as only an Irishman can be, and male. He was Mrs. Tappan's brother. A stone mason or, as he preferred, a bricklayer.

On Saturday mornings Unkie used to come to our apartment, bringing us treats from Eastern Market. We would hear the door at the top of the steps opening, and then, with a "hint of Irish laughter" Unkie's voice would ring out. "Little gypsy dandelion, now I mow you down." Always the same.

A senseless, whimsical greeting that none of us really understood, but all of us found hilarious. Maybe it was just the delight of being embraced by Unkie's caring. He was our own beloved leprechaun.

From out of a big paper bag would come the Kaiser rolls, the doughnuts, chocolate fudge, liverwurst – whatever had caught his eye at the market. Sometimes we had an instant picnic right there on the dining room table – all from Unkie's gifts of the day.

Unkie smoked cigarettes. Rolled his own. He choreographed every move, put his whole body into it. We all watched, fascinated. First, he took out one cigarette paper from a small stack. Then he pulled a tobacco pouch from his pocket and tapped a small amount of sweet-smelling tobacco (yes, that evil weed did smell sweet, no matter how lethal) onto the paper with his index finger. He closed the pouch's drawstring with his teeth.

To seal the paper shut after rolling it up, he licked it lengthwise. Actually, it was more like a caress. And even though that cigarette had been made with such tender care, it still looked thin and flimsy, as if it would collapse at any minute. But it never did. He lit it with a deft scratch of a match, his hand cupped around the flame.

He didn't take many puffs, once the carefully executed structure was completed. Maybe putting it together was the best part. It was for us.

When referring to Mr. Tappan, Granny invariably added, "You can set your watch by him." He worked at the Government Printing Office, less than a mile from home. He walked, of course. Everybody did, except Papa and Mr. Puglisi and Mr. Johnny and Dr. Jaeger. They lived over their businesses and went downstairs to work, as did a large number of men on Capitol Hill in the Twenties. Very few of the women worked outside the home.

If we got up early enough while staying at Granny's, we could see Margaret and Stella, the two older Tappan girls, come out of the house on the way to Mass every morning at St. Peter's, down on Second Street below Pennsylvania Avenue.

And if we were up late enough on Friday or Saturday night, we could see them coming home with their dates, after a night of dancing at Wardman Park Hotel or some other highly fashionable night spot. They had beautiful clothes, and I thought they were very glamorous.

Nora was Brother's age, and was tolerant enough to play with me sometimes in my doll's house. If she was around at dinner time, and we asked her to stay for dinner, she invariably asked what we were having. If it were Thursday (Oscie's half-day off) and Mama was doing her one and only specialty of steak and French fries, Nora stayed. Otherwise, she would turn down the invitation with an "I think I hear my mother calling me."

I wasn't aware of the family's social life, except for a few places that we visited.

Occasionally we "took tea" at Cousin Wilbur's – he of the pearl-gray spats and year-round white outfits. He and his sisters and niece lived in a classy home in the LeDroit Park neighborhood, a little northeast of Howard University. The house sat sidewise on a hill overlooking the lake-like reservoir ("the reservoy" to native Washingtonians).

A wide-terraced lawn graced the side of the lot, guarded over by the longest porch I had ever seen. A freshly painted railing stretched its entire length. In my memory it was always wet. "Mind the railing," Cousin Wilbur used to call out. "Wet paint." He seemed to say it each time we visited. Cousin Wilbur was the sort of person who warned children not to breathe in his presence. And I think we obeyed.

The exterior of this mansion (at least in my eyes) was impressive. But the inside left me slack-jawed.

They had a *dumbwaiter* connecting the downstairs, English basement kitchen to the huge dining room, at street level. It had two shelves, and moved on thick ropes.

As Cousin Wilbur was showing off the wonders of this domestic novelty, Brother was climbing aboard. Mama and Cousin Wilbur lunged to grab him, but Cousin Wilbur was quicker, and soon had him in his clutches, upright and harmless.

Brother said afterwards that this distant cousin had pinched him through his thick wool jacket.

The last we saw of them – Cousin Wilbur and his non-nuclear family – they were living on Capitol Hill, in another spectacular house. This one was on B Street, S.E. (now Independence Avenue), where one of the House Office Buildings stands today.

Overlooking the entire living room was a second-floor, railed balcony. Quite handsome. Awesome.

Did I mention that the front parlor of the LeDroit Park residence was furnished in oh-so-delicate Louis XVI gilded chairs, upholstered in pink and powder-blue fabrics?

Après moi, le Rayburn Building.

CHAPTER 11

GLEN ECHO AND THE CORCORAN

The streetcar to Glen Echo Amusement Park didn't go up East Capitol. We had to change cars. On sultry hot nights, Mama and Brother and I often made the trip to catch whatever summer breeze there was. We waited for the open cars with no walls.

It was a great ride, through town and out into the country, with tree limbs and bushes brushing against the ends of the seats that went crosswise across the car. As we drew close to Glen Echo, the streetcar rattled over an open trestle that looked as fragile as if it were made of matchsticks, and I held my breath.

"Glen Echo," the conductor called, and everybody got off but us. We stayed on to Cabin John, the end of the line, just a few minutes away.

The conductor would switch the seats to face in the other direction, and then walk to the (now) front and man the controls there.

Brother would start begging when we reached the trestle on the way in. "Why *can't* I go to Glen Echo?" he'd nag as only a ten-, eleven-, twelve-year old can nag. Papa was gone now and our mother was sometimes overwhelmed with the responsibility of handling this young buck.

"Gee," he'd whine. "You don't let me do *anything*. What are you afraid I'll do? Fall out of the Ferris wheel? Stand up in the roller coaster? Why don't you let me go, Mom? Huh? Why not?"

She would look pained, and just promise, "When you get old enough." Sometimes she added, almost to herself, *if only he had a man to go with him.* Roller coasters and Ferris wheels were outside her comfort zone. They were Brother's most desirable danger.

I got to go to the park once. My grandfather's youngest sister took me. Since Grandpap was the oldest and Aunt Susie the youngest of twelve, she was close to Mama's age when we went.

We did the tame things: rode the merry-go-round, laughed at ourselves in crazy mirrors, and walked over floors that zigzagged under our feet. Then we got sticky from cotton candy. I thought it was exciting.

It didn't take much to thrill me. A low-maintenance kid.

Eventually, I'm sure Brother went with his teenaged pals, though I don't remember hearing anything about the adventure. I do remember, though, the increasingly heated debates about letting colored people into Glen Echo. The swimming pool especially was at the center of dissention. I was an adult by this time.

After several years of standoff, African Americans entered the park as well as the pool. The whites who wanted to deny them entry claimed that "they took over, just as we said they would."

The whole time that whites had been filling Glen Echo Amusement Park, I never heard anyone say that whites were taking over. Why was that?

Among my favorite outings was visiting the Corcoran Gallery of Art with Mama, before the National Gallery was even thought of by Mr. Mellon.

Our first stop, just inside the entrance, was the life-sized *Pieta*. Mama always lifted me up so that I could get the full view of this Michelangelo masterpiece of the youthful Virgin holding the crucified body of her son, the Christ, in her arms.

When I was fully grown, I learned that the Corcoran *Pieta* was a superb copy, but not the original (which, of course, is at the Vatican). Its value was not diminished one iota in my eyes.

Another large marble piece of art there also left its mark on my consciousness for the rest of my life – *The Dying Gaul*, a tousle-haired, muscular warrior, supporting himself on one arm as he valiantly breathes his last. Around his neck is a torque or circlet.

Mama explained that such jewelry was common hundreds of years ago and was usually made of fine gold.

I thought it was a very strange thing for a man – and a warrior, to boot – to wear gold jewelry. Imagine a man in a necklace! But that was a long time ago. What would I have thought if he had been wearing diamond earrings?

When I saw a photo of this Gaul in Thomas Cahill's *How the Irish Saved Civilization*, I welcomed him back in my life as an old friend. My friend in a gold necklace.

These two works of art grew on me the way great music becomes more endearing with repeated listening. I didn't think of the subjects as depressing at all. Maybe that was because I was introduced to some real downers at birth, literally.

I was born at Granny's house on A Street between a steel engraving on one side of the bed titled *Pour le Pauvre*, depicting pitifully maimed wretches in togas begging at the Roman Forum, and on the other side of the bed, an oil painting of Charlotte Corday in prison. She had just murdered her lover in the bathtub. This had happened during the French Revolution. His name was Marat. Aunt

Gertie told me about them. So I was well prepared for the *Pieta* and *The Dying Gaul*.

Further along at the Corcoran were the exciting *Horse Fair* picture by Rosa Bonheur and some lovely ladies painted by Madame Vigee LeBrun. Mama made sure that I pronounced the names of both artists with the proper accent and deep-throated, gargled French "r." She also never failed to impress on me the fact that they were *women*. Every bit as good as the male artists.

Once we got to my very favorite picture in the entire gallery, though, Mama had the sense to be quiet and leave me to my own adoration. Compared to many other works of art at the Corcoran, this one had no great claims to fame. But I loved it for what it meant to me.

A very large picture, it is an oil of a weathered old fisherman working one oar of a rowboat. Beside him, and looking up at his face with complete trust is a little girl – probably about my age when I first saw it. That would be four or five. With her hand on the other oar, she's helping him row the boat.

It's titled *The Helping Hand*.

I identified with that little girl. She was helping someone she loved, helping him to do something that he couldn't do without her. Or that's how I saw it. Maybe I desperately wanted to be needed.

As life crowded in, and I did become needed, the National Gallery of Art came between me and the Corcoran and the little "helping hand." I lost track of her, but I never completely forgot her.

The National Gallery's *Head of a Little Boy* by Desiderio di Settignano came close to superseding all other works of art in my affection until the day I walked into the newly refurbished Renwick Gallery. And there she was. Twice as big as life, and still beaming up at the fisherman with delight. The "helping hand" was still needed.

Mama and I often went to the theater to see something utterly inappropriate for a small child, but unforgettable. We went to the matinee show, which was usually a series of short skits or one-act plays. One afternoon we saw some Russian actress named Alla Nazimova in a short but violent drama during which she shot off a very loud pistol. I responded with a very loud scream.

I can remember being carried up the aisle, still screaming, over Mama's shoulder, facing the actress, who was standing stock still on the stage, looking daggers at me.

The only musical matinee I remember was an orchestral one, featuring Schubert's *Unfinished Symphony*. Mama told me about Schubert's misfortune to be in love with someone who didn't love him. I thought that was sad – until I came across a pencil sketch of Franz Schubert in the program. Although I still felt sorry for him, I understood better why this girl didn't want to marry him. He wasn't my type, either.

When the Oberammergau Passion Play came to Washington, our extended family filled an entire row, down front in orchestra seats. Although the actors spoke their lines in German, I knew the plot and didn't need any translation, even though some great aunt or great uncle on whose lap I was sitting insisted on interpreting the action for me.

At the Crucifixion scene, a most peculiar thing happened. The "good thief" who was crucified beside Christ says a few lines in defense of Him. I didn't speak or understand a word of German – except that I understood every word that the "good thief" said. No, I didn't hear it in my memory from scripture readings at church. What I heard wasn't in the Elizabethan English of the

King James Bible. In fact, I didn't consciously *hear* it at all. I was instantaneously receiving the message sent out by this man, without needing a translation.

It was a preview of the feeling I had in the reading room of the Library of Congress, where I was laboriously reading a book in French by André Gide and translating it for a report due the next day. Suddenly I was turning the pages at high speed – as if I had shifted gears. I *had* shifted *mental* gears, and – a miracle – was at last thinking in French.

I had somehow shifted into German at the Passion Play. German or telepathy.

Something similar occurred when Granny took me to see a Mary Pickford movie. It was still the era of silent films, with captions on the screen. Granny was reading them to me as I knelt on the seat beside her. But I waved her aside. I could tell what Mary Pickford was saying before Granny could read the words.

I was reading her lips. Effortlessly.

Just Mary Pickford's lips. I couldn't read anyone else's.

My family was astounded. It was as if we had a talking dog.

And somewhere in my childhood I heard the voice of Miss Ethyl Barrymore reaching across the footlights to me as she spoke the line, "That's all there is; there isn't any more."

There hasn't ever been any moment in any theater to surpass that moment for me.

CHAPTER 12

TRIPS TO VIRGINIA AND
MARYLAND BY CAR

About the only place where we were invited out to dinner was an apartment a few doors down Third Street in the home of two of my favorite people, Mr. Pettus and Mr. Beatty.

Mr. Pettus was rector of our church, St. Mark's, at Third and A Streets, S.E. In that era Episcopalians called their clergy Mister – in the English way. Well, Low Church and Broad Church (medium rare) Episcopalians did. If you wanted High Church Anglican, you went to St. James up on Eighth Street, N.E., for smells and bells (incense and sanctus bell), and you called the clergyman Father. At St. James, he was a priest. At St. Mark's, he was a minister. And all clergy, High, Broad, or Low, were "he." It would take a long time for *her* to become an Episcopal priest. But *she* made it, after all.

Papa was a very devout Episcopalian, who used to "slip over" to St. James occasionally for early Mass. There was a saying in the family that many of us "leaned toward High Church but none of us fell in."

When we got together with Mr. Pettus and his friend, Mr. Beatty, they left church talk at the door, and we had wide-ranging conversation and much laughter.

Mr. Pettus had a clean-shaven, open face, and a radiant smile. He was rather stout, but when he flung that dramatic cape over his broad shoulders, he looked positively dashing. Mr. Beatty, who either shared the rectory with Mr. Pettus or visited often – I don't know which – was trim and sported a mustache. Or that's the way I can see him in memory.

They both paid a lot of attention to me, and I lapped up the special treatment.

The first time we went to their place for dinner, Mr. Beatty, a gourmet cook, went to the kitchen shortly after we arrived and emerged with a plate of hot *hors d'oeuvres*, which he placed on a table near where I was standing. And which I devoured almost instantly.

I knew I had done something wrong when Brother sidled up to Mama and whispered to her. She looked over at me, eyes wide, her nose doing the rabbit twitch – a rare sign of disapproval.

"Oh, Sissy," she wailed. "Those were meant for ..."

Mr. Beatty cut in. "Those were meant for her," he said. "There are plenty more in the kitchen." Then he looked straight at me and said he was delighted that I enjoyed his cooking so much.

Eager to please him even more, when we were seated at the dinner table, I speared a fancy little yellow ball from a side dish and ate it, accompanied by rolled eyeballs and feigned rapture. It was a butterball. My first.

At least once, Mr. Pettus and Mr. Beatty took the whole family – including Granny – on a picnic "down into" Virginia. Or it could have been "out into" Maryland. (Virginia was always "down" and we'd go "out" into Maryland.)

We rode in an open touring car – with a roof, but open sides. The picnic was probably in the Arlington open countryside. Or maybe out near that isolated crossroad Georgia Avenue (Seventh Street or Brookeville Road) and Bladensburg Road (University

Boulevard) where there was a wooden sign that read "Wheaton – the Community of Tomorrow." And we all used to laugh. I wish we had bought an acre or two in that wilderness.

Mr. Pettus had an occasional stammer, which he controlled somewhat by emphasizing certain words. In the *Sursum Corda*, for instance, I used to wait for the part where (using the 1925 Prayer Book) he would say, "It is VERY MEET, right, and our BOUND-EN DUTY, that we should at all TIMES, and in all PLACES, give THANKS unto thee ...."

CHAPTER 13

RED CARPET TREATMENT

The day Mr. Pettus took me to the Big Event, he didn't stammer at all. It was right after Christmas of 1924 – as I remember it. I was dressed in a red raincoat with a hood, and wearing red Wellington boots. I took Mr. Pettus' hand as he led me to the streetcar stop at Third and East Capitol. My family and the "men downstairs" were all standing at an office plate glass window, waving goodbye.

I was four, about to turn five, and I had never been away from home with anyone outside the family. But that was not why the assembled multitude was waving me goodbye. Mr. Pettus was taking me someplace special. Everybody else seemed to know where we were going, but I hadn't a clue. I must have trusted Mr. Pettus because I wasn't scared. And I remember being aware of the fact that I wasn't scared. That seemed peculiar to me. Strange child.

It was a bitterly cold day, with sleet and freezing rain pelting the streetcar windows. We went past the Capitol, around to Union Station, and into downtown, where I looked for – and found – my favorite landmark along the route. Sometimes I missed it, when Mama and I took the streetcar down to Woodies store or the National Theater. But on this trip, there it was – in a little shop in a squarish display window on the second floor.

The display was simple: A free-standing artificial leg that went up to hip level. A cardboard cutout of a blond, curly-haired little girl was hugging the limb, and a balloon that emerged from her head said, in big letters, "My daddy's leg is a Universal." I loved it.

I really was an odd child.

Another favorite attraction of this ride was gone that day because of the weather. The gypsy palm readers and fortune tellers who used to sit out in front of their signs at tiny shops all along the north side of Pennsylvania Avenue were missing. In summer, the women in their colorful, full-skirted dresses and big, hoop earrings would call out to passersby, trying to entice them to get their fortunes told or their palms read. Or whatever. They were far more alluring than the J. Edgar Hoover Building or the Canadian Embassy of today's Avenue.

When Mr. Pettus and I got to our destination, I took a pratfall on the ice right in front of a big iron gate. My pride was hurt, but nothing else was. The next thing I remember was standing on a red carpet in front of – almost on top of – a pair of the most bulbous-toed shoes I'd ever seen. Mr. Pettus and the man wearing the shoes were talking. He called Mr. Pettus "Billy." Mr. Pettus called him "Mr. President."

Then the two heads were leaning down, close to mine. "Mr. President" said something about my being "Little Red Riding Hood," and he gently pushed the hood back off my face. Immediately, I pulled it down again. I sensed that something important was going on here, and just a piece of it was as much as I could handle. "Mr. President" was being very gentle and trying to get me to talk. I felt so sorry for him, but it was impossible for me to do anything more than stare at those round-topped shoes and avoid eye contact.

When we got back home, everybody pelted me with questions.

"Did he say anything to you?"

"I bet he didn't."

"Did he shake your hand?"

"What did he look like?"

I didn't answer any of their questions. They wouldn't understand that quiet, soft-spoken man who tried so hard to get me to talk.

So I remained silent.

"In her Grandma Zurhorst mood," Mama sighed.

Mr. Pettus and this gentle man, I learned many years later, had been fast friends back home in Massachusetts, and had remained close after the friend became President of the United States. He was Calvin Coolidge, and we had been to his first New Year's Day reception.

CHAPTER 14

MISERABLE OFFENSES
AT ST. MARK'S

From the beginning, I got off on the wrong foot at St. Mark's, the Episcopal Church at Third and A Streets, S.E., one block from our place.

I understand that it's not the church now that it was when we attended it in the Twenties – Mama singing in the choir and often doing solos and duets, Papa teaching Sunday school to young men and serving on the vestry, Brother attending Sunday school, and me screaming bloody hell to stay out of it altogether.

Near the top of a pile of unforgettable childhood memories is my grabbing every rung of every iron fence between our place and St. Mark's – and every house had an iron fence – loudly protesting my forced attendance at Sunday school.

As whoever in charge of me at the moment pried my fingers loose from each upright, I'd swing on to the next one and scream louder.

Finally, we would arrive at the "valley of the shadow of death," which was at the foot of the steep, interminable wooden stairway in the old parish hall. The stairs didn't frighten me; it was the terrifying old man at the very top who turned my stomach and made my blood run cold.

He had a long, full white beard and a booming voice which would come thundering down that enclosed stairwell to ask me – by name, like the angel of death – why I hadn't been to Sunday school for the past three Sundays. I was a four- or five-year-old child, for heaven's sake. "Do you have a WRITTEN EXCUSE, Mary Zurhorst?"

My memories of those encounters couldn't be accurate; I'm now getting the nightmare version. In it, I'm always alone, tiny, shaking with terror, head downcast at the foot of the abyss, as that vengeful, Old Testament prophet – Elijah? Elisha? – hurled lightning bolts down at me. It was Elisha, wasn't it, who cursed the little boys ("in the name of the Lord!") when they called him a "baldhead," and then he smiled smugly (inferred) when two she-bears tore up 42 of the boys? I've learned these horrors as a grownup, and applied them to my nemesis. At the time, I thought he was Moses. Or God.

There were other problems at St. Mark's – of my own doing. At a too-tender age I was a flower girl in a wedding there. The rehearsal went well, as I pantomimed tossing loose rose petals up the aisle. The actual roses handed to me in a basket on the day of the wedding were still firmly intact, however, every petal still attached. Nobody seemed to notice.

The wedding march started with the familiar fanfare, and I led the wedding party two steps up the aisle. Then I stopped, pulled and tugged at the roses, which were not coming apart. So, finding that the job took two hands, I sat down in the aisle and proceeded to dismantle – or un-petal – every rose in the basket. After frantic milling about of the wedding party when I refused to budge, they went on without me. Eventually, somebody picked me up and took me home, with me protesting I wasn't finished yet.

Me in my flower girl dress, made by Granny.

In another fiasco at St. Mark's, there I was at a church social –
Dutch bob, mouse-brown hair, squinty eyes and dour mouth at
about age five – on the stage of the parish hall, belting out "Jesus
Wants Me for a Sunbeam" or something of that ilk. When the last,
tuneless note hit the rafters, the audience politely applauded. The
response overwhelmed me. They liked me! So I did an encore for
which the church pianist kindly accompanied me again. I vaguely
recall hearing my name called from off-stage, but I ignored it.
Couldn't they see that I was performing?

I was still singing when my father literally dragged me from
the stage. "But they want more," I tried to explain. Papa didn't
understand.

And for a long time, nobody seemed to understand the harm
that dreadful man at the top of the stairs was doing to my psyche.
Also, my performance rating was hitting new lows, as I flubbed
each appearance at parish social events, no matter how undemand-
ing my role was.

Eventually, I was removed from performing and – Hallelujah! –
taken out of Sunday school permanently. I went to church instead.
That experience enriched my life beyond measure.

I couldn't read yet, so the majestic language of the King James
Bible and the heavenly cadences of Archbishop Thomas Cranmer's
Book of Common Prayer flowed into my soul like water filling an
empty pool. I gradually and naturally memorized what I heard, and
the words have never left me.

Through the Liturgy (rites and services) at St. Mark's I was
introduced to the "beauty of holiness" of the Old and New Testament as well as such prayers as the opening of the Communion
service: *"Almighty God, unto whom all hearts are open, all desires
known, and from whom no secrets are hid, cleanse the thoughts*

of our hearts with the inspiration of thy Holy Spirit that we may perfectly love thee and worthily magnify thy holy name, through Christ Our Lord, Amen."

The English language doesn't get much better than that.

I fell in love with the poetry, the sheer beauty of the words, the lilting cadence of the Elizabethan masterpiece of literature that is the Anglican *Book of Common Prayer.*

Although I tolerate many of the modern revisions, I found one deletion unforgivable: the arguably most ancient and most beautiful benediction ever written. It is the Aaronic Blessing, attributed to Aaron, the High Priest, brother of Moses. I'm told that it is now missing from the Prayer Book because it is not Trinitarian. Bad cess to those tone-dead, soul-dead, overzealous bean counters who threw it out. It never failed to make me feel truly blessed – directly by God.

"The Lord bless you and keep you. The Lord make his face to shine upon you and be gracious unto you. The Lord lift up the light of his countenance upon you and give you peace, now and forevermore. Amen."

May it rise again to feed the souls of those yet to come.

Several years after I had moved away and transferred my membership from St. Mark's to a suburban church, I found my St. Mark's demon lying in wait for me. My brother, who then was living at 301 East Capitol and teaching junior high school-age boys at Sunday school, had the flu. He asked me to take his place in church that Easter Sunday, sitting with the class as they placed flowers in the Easter cross on the chancel steps.

I was reluctant, remembering old disasters at St. Mark's.

"Nothing could go wrong," Brother said. "All you have to do is just sit there."

The boys were given flowers as they entered the church, and by the time they reached our pew, they were griping about getting daisies when others had Easter lilies or roses. When it came their turn to put the flowers in the cross, I noticed that each boy was doing a funny little sleight-of-hand trick, and coming back with a wide grin.

As each one returned to the pew, he opened his fist and dropped a rose on my lap. Pretty soon, I had a lap overflowing with roses.

The cross had a gaping hole where they had come from.

I could almost hear a demonic voice purring, "Welcome back, Mary Zurhorst."

I hear that St. Mark's is very different now. It's gone from low-church conservative, deeply traditional, to an avant-garde style which allows modern plays to be performed in the nave. They'd have dancing in the aisles if they had aisles – but they took out the pews. And they do all sorts of social outreach now, to help the community and the world. Best of all, Elisha is gone.

St. Mark's is surely not the church I knew in the early Twenties. Thanks be to God!

CHAPTER 15

A NON-CATHOLIC AT ST. CECILIA'S

St. Cecilia's was just three blocks down East Capitol Street from where we lived. I was sent to this Roman Catholic Academy for girls, not only because it was close, but also because it was a "safe" place. And it had a good reputation. The Holy Cross nuns ran it.

I was its only Protestant.

For the first few years I had one friend among the students: Leicester Higgins.

He was its only boy.

The girls gathered in little groups, looking at me and making audible remarks about the peculiarities of my faith, as they perceived it. "They don't believe in the Blessed Mother," was a favorite comment. "Do you think she'll go to Purgatory?" was another. Some were betting on my going straight to hell.

Actually, I didn't do much to make friends with them, either. I had never had a playmate of my own age, and suddenly I was in the midst of all these alien creatures. I was terrified.

When my last pencil was bitten down to a pulp, I sought refuge in the deep folds of Sister Benigna's black robes and found comfort in her warm embrace. I can still feel those wooden rosary beads up against my cheek. They hung from her waist.

The day started at St. Cecilia's with a class recitation of "Hail, Holy Queen," a prayer we said at breakneck speed, and (for me) complete lack of comprehension. The words blurred as they flew past. "... moaning, weakness, valley of tears ...."

We then recited the name of the Apostolic Delegate (now called Papal Nuncio from the Vatican) to the United States. "Pietro Fumasoni Biondi," we shouted out in unison. It is forever engraved on my mind. R.I.P.

St. Cecilia's was a bit heavy on "churchy" things; a bit light on the Sermon on the Mount and forgiveness.

At the end of the school day, we marched up to the chapel to say the rosary. For whatever reason, by my second or third year there, I became the leader in this devotion, and was proud to do it.

But I missed Jesus.

My friend Leicester had an endearing habit of dropping little confidences to me as he passed my desk; such memorable sayings as, "Mary Teresa smells like crushed beetles." And she did.

He could pull this off without moving his lips, so Sister never suspected anything.

Everybody pronounced his name as Leecester. Except my mother. "Ask him if his family calls him Lester," Mama told me. "That's an English name. It's not pronounced Leecester."

I asked him, and he said my mother was right. He confessed he was letting the nuns get away with the mistake, just to have his own, inside joke. "They don't know no better," he grinned. He also liked to shock the nuns by using outrageous grammar.

In the third or fourth grade we were assigned to write an essay about a visit to the home of the "Blessed Mother" and the young Jesus. The girls read aloud pious details of the visit, describing

Jesus's home, which was decorated with pictures of a bleeding Sacred Heart, crucifixes and flickering candles at shrines to the Blessed Virgin Mary and the Little Flower (St. Teresa of Lisieux) throughout the house.

When it came time for Leicester to read his essay, a great silence fell across the room, in anticipation of what we all knew would be a different approach to the subject. Sister Mary Frances stroked nervously at the replica of the Sacred Heart that fell from her broad starched collar.

Leicester rose from his desk and began to read. The words are etched on my mind.

"Well, Leicester, you sure are a sight for sore eyes," Mary said when she saw me coming. She was out in the yard, slopping the hogs.

"Where's Jesus?"

"He's down at the swimming hole, skinny-dipping with some other little Jewish boys. Why don't you join them? You can leave your clothes here." Leicester took his seat.

There was a nervous clapping of a few hands, which stopped almost before it began. Sister's lips were quivering, her bountiful chest heaving beneath the stiff collar. Finally, her laughter burst loose. And, of course, as soon as the class saw Sister's reaction, we all felt free to follow along. Leicester stood and bowed, a wry grin on his face.

Even though Leicester and I were friends, he wasn't the kind of pal whose house I went to, or who came to mine. There was no one like that at St. Cecilia's until I was in about the third grade, and Hermia Frances Healy transferred in to my school.

Hermie, as she was called, was blonde and pretty, a Ginger Rogers type. She had class. Not my kind of friend at all, I thought, as I looked her over.

After a couple of weeks at St. Cecilia's, she came over to me one day. "I told my mother about you," she said without the usual awkwardness of breaking the ice. "She said it's all right for us to be friends. She knows about you and she doesn't mind."

Hermie didn't have to explain; I knew what she meant: I was a Protestant in a Catholic school in the 1920s.

"My father was a Protestant before he married Mother, and he converted. So we understand. Oh," she quickly added, "I don't mean you should convert. It's perfectly all right with us for you to be ... whatever you are. We can be friends, if you want to be."

I wanted to be. Very much. And so we were – for the next 30 years, until she died of cancer in California, the wife of a naval officer and mother of two sons. And beloved friend.

There were times when I argued with the nuns – politely, doggedly. I must have been a thorn in their side.

"But Sister, when we say the prayers so fast, we can't know what we're saying."

"That doesn't matter. What counts is that you are saying the prayers, and every time you say the 'Hail, Holy Queen,' for example, you get time off in Purgatory. This is called an indulgence."

"But that's not why you say prayers, Sister. You don't do it for credit."

No matter what the subject, I was always dismissed with the same explanation: "Well, you wouldn't understand, dear, because you're not a Catholic."

It was quite a challenge. One way that I met that challenge was to practically memorize the *Baltimore Catechism*. Mainly, I wanted to show them at St. Cecilia's that Protestants were every bit as Christian as they were, and not bound for either Purgatory or Hell just because of their beliefs. My efforts were futile, but worthy. Actually, I have never believed in either place, but I couldn't go so far as to tell them *that*.

After six years of the *Baltimore Catechism* (I skipped two grades early on), I realize in retrospect that the most important lesson that I learned from that book was the difference between the Immaculate Conception and the Virgin Birth. I'd say that over half of lifelong Roman Catholics get it wrong – if asked. And nearly all of the Protestants, though chances of their being asked at all are slim.

For the record: the Immaculate Conception is the Roman Catholic doctrine that the Virgin Mary was conceived in her mother's womb, free from all stain of original sin. The Virgin Birth is the doctrine that Jesus was miraculously begotten by God and born of Mary, who was a virgin.

You never know when such information will come in handy.

My mother's uninhibited behavior with the nuns was an embarrassment to me at St. Cecilia's. Since she wasn't Roman Catholic, she didn't know how to act with them.

I could tell whenever she came into the building; there was that kind of twittering you hear when a flock of birds lands in a tree. Sometimes a nun would call out, "Edwinetta's here," and teachers would leave classrooms and squeal (yes, actually squeal) as they ran toward her. Up and down the hall were cries of, "Oh, you brought my hair clippers!" "Manicure scissors, just what I wanted." "How did you know I needed Pond's Cold Cream? My hands have been so chapped."

There was lots of laughter in the hall, imitated by my classmates. They would do pretend hugs and kisses and ape the voices: "Oooh, Edwinetta, you brought me that lipstick I needed!" "How did you know I had been praying for hair curlers?"

How I wished that Mama were more like Mrs. Colliflower, a proper Roman Catholic matron who had two girls at St. Cecilia's, and knew how to treat nuns – with calm dignity and respect. Mrs. Colliflower was married to Mr. Colliflower who was a well known coal and wood (and, later, oil) merchant in D.C.

When she visited St. Cecilia's, Mrs. Colliflower was a model of propriety – fox scarf draped just so, around her neck, the fox's jaw clamping down on the upper end of the tail. Understated string of, I'm sure, real pearls adorning the proper white blouse of her classic black suit. Sensible Cuban heels, as befits a woman of her position. Unobtrusive hat, with an upturned brim and small feather.

My mother wore none of the above. I couldn't vouch for what she did wear, but I know it was more informal than Mrs. Colliflower's. It was embarrassing to hear the nuns carrying on like that when she visited. Once or twice – for just a second – I wished Mrs. Colliflower were my mother.

I told Sister Lenore how I felt. I could tell her anything. She was my art teacher, and held forth in a little, cramped studio separate from the school building because it had a kiln in it that heated up to frighteningly high temperatures in order to fire the iridescent dishes and gold demitasse cups and saucers we painted. We also did some still-lifes in water colors.

When she wasn't teaching art to her students and listening to their troubles, Sister Lenore fluted the bonnets of these Holy Cross nuns. The linen headdresses gave the effect of wide, white rays emanating from the nuns' faces. The bonnets arrived at her studio in buckets, laundered and damp with thick starch, several in each bucket, and many buckets. In the studio was a machine with long metal rods clustered together and a foot treadle. As my deeply loved Sister Lenore and I talked, she threaded the limp, wet linen in and out, around the rods. This took a while. So we could talk.

Her favorite subject was ghosts. I had heard a few choice ghost stories, and loved to tell them to her.

"So Mama and Papa were at this séance, and the medium was angry at Papa because Papa had gotten down on the floor in the dark and grabbed Mama's ankle, and Mama screamed. Papa didn't believe in the spirit world, and Mama did. Anyway, the medium said she had a message for Papa if he would behave. It was from a girl he had gone with before he met Mama, and the girl had died, and her body had been at the funeral parlors. With no one else in the room, Papa had slipped a small flower into her hand and said he was sorry he couldn't have loved her more, and gave her a kiss on the cheek.

"The medium quoted his words verbatim, and said the girl wanted to tell him she appreciated what he did."

Sister applied a quick step to the treadle. There was a big hiss of steam, and the bonnet stiffened up as if touched by magic.

"It's the work of the devil, it is," said Sister Lenore. "But tell me more."

I learned more about human caring and compassion and Christian kindness in those years in the studio with Sister Lenore than I did from six years of the *Baltimore Catechism*.

One unfortunate nun, recently transferred into St. Cecilia's, was given the thankless job of trying to teach me to play the piano.

With all of the professional musicians in my mother's family, you would think that I would have inherited one small chromosome of musical talent, but it all went to my brother, who, strangely, wasn't made to study music.

At my third or fourth lesson, metronome clicking back and forth like a bobblehead on top of the upright piano, I painfully picked out a few notes, ignoring the metronome – and indeed, the notes on the sheet music. It was "Poupèe Dansant" that I was supposed to be playing, ironically. My version sounded more like "Dead Doll."

"What do you think you're doing?" Sister Philomena (or whatever her name was) asked, genuinely puzzled. "You haven't practiced, have you?"

"No, Sister, I haven't." Unrepentant.

"And why not?"

"There's a body downstairs, Sister."

She stiffened. She began fingering the rosary beads at her waist. "A body downstairs? What kind of a body?"

"A dead body, Sister." Matter-of-fact.

"Are you speaking in this manner of a dearly departed member of your family who has died?" She crossed herself, gasping, "Jesus, Mary and Joseph." (I made a mental note to explain to her later that these weren't the usual words for the sign of the cross, but let it go for now.)

"No, Sister. I don't know who it is. They bring them to our place – usually late at night, and then we bury them."

She retreated to the one window in the room, where she stood, shoulders heaving. And then she turned. "SHUT OFF THAT METRONOME!" she shrieked, at the breaking point.

Within moments, she had me by the shoulders, marching me to the office of Sister Prudenciana, the Mother Superior. Without knocking, she barged in, bursting with outrage. The words tumbled out in a deluge.

Instead of fear, I felt a great calm – as I always did in the presence of this magnificent woman who was in charge of St. Cecilia's Academy and the convent. What's more, I noticed that she still had, on her desk, the bookends my mother had given her at Christmas – Dante and Beatrice. They delighted her. I will always remember what she said when Mama presented them to her. "Oh, Edwinetta, if we had been living in the Middle Ages, we would have been hussies, wouldn't we!"

At the time I was scandalized. My mother was leading astray the Mother Superior!

Now, here in her office, watching her smile grow wider and wider as my music teacher recited my shocking story, I waited to hear what she would say. I couldn't understand what was wrong.

The story told, Mother Prudenciana reached out and drew me into her arms, as she chuckled softly. "Tell her, dear, tell Sister about your family business."

I had never before been asked to do that. "We have an undertaking parlor," I said.

Fuming, my music teacher asked me why I hadn't told her.

"I thought everybody knew," I said.

With a grin, the Mother Superior turned to me. "Sister is from Philadelphia, dear." That explained everything.

CHAPTER 16

MEETING LINDBERGH - ALMOST

I was awakened by Fred's voice in the hall of our apartment. "Get Sissy up," he said. "Lindbergh's at Bolling Field. I want to take her over there to meet him." (I have no idea how Fred knew Lindbergh would be at Bolling Field.)

Fred was one of the "men downstairs" who worked for the business, and was a family favorite. He was young, blond and witty. And caring. I had a big crush on Fred. And, of course, Lindbergh was my idol.

The prospect of meeting the most famous man in the world should have thrilled me more than it did. I kept wondering what this eight-year old girl could possibly say or do that would matter to this superhero.

"Aren't you excited?" Fred asked me in the car on the way to Bolling Field, across the Anacostia. He sensed something was missing in my reaction.

"Sure," I answered. How could I explain that I wanted to meet Charles Augustus Lindbergh more than anybody else in the universe? But why would he want to meet me?

I grinned a faked joyful anticipation all the way up to the moment we encountered the Man himself, standing next to a small plane with two or three other men around him.

Oh, no, I prayed, recoiling. Inside my head I was pleading, *Please, Fred, no. Can't you see he's thinking? Don't make me intrude on his private thoughts. Please. Leave him alone.*

Fred Stuart, who worked for the business, holding a picture and bust of Charles Lindbergh soon after we had gone to Bolling Field to meet him.

And then I could feel Fred's hand at my back, as he thrust me toward the most celebrated person alive.

"Colonel Lindbergh," I heard Fred say, "would you shake hands with my little friend here? She idolizes you."

I wanted to run as far away as possible.

Lindbergh, completely focused on the job at hand and oblivious to Fred and me, walked up to the propeller and leaned hard on it several times, until the motor caught, and it began to spin. He quickly climbed into the cockpit.

"Sonofabitch." Fred's face was red with rage. "It wouldn't have hurt him to shake your hand." Fred put his arm around me. "I'm sorry, Sissy. I guess fame's gone to his head."

Instinctively, I knew that fame hadn't gone to Lindbergh's head. It had been this ability to concentrate, to stay committed to the task, single-minded, uninterruptible, that brought fame to him. It was what had enabled him to fly a tiny airplane, solo, nonstop across the Atlantic Ocean. It was this talent to wall out distraction that *made* him famous.

Such rare heroes are better left alone.

CHAPTER 17

LIFE BEFORE CHOLESTEROL

If it weren't for the frozen macaroon mint ball with hot fudge sauce, the autumn ritual of trying on skirts and blouses and dresses and "underbodies" would have been intolerable.

My mother had favorite salesladies in each department at Woodward & Lothrop's Department Store – women who seemed to commit their lives to their jobs and were there year after year. Mama would phone days ahead of our visit and ask the clerk to choose outfits for me, and have them ready when we arrived. They were to be "in tones of brown or green, because those are her colors."

I got so tired of those colors that I still don't have a brown or green thread in my closet.

But I never tired of the frozen macaroon mint balls with hot fudge sauce served in Woodies' Tea Room later. This scrumptious dessert topped off a chicken salad to die for, and was in a league only with the chicken salad offered by Avignon Frères, which reigned at 18th and Columbia Road, N.W.

Was the food actually better when I was seven, eight, nine years old? Or was my palate so innocent then that everything just tasted better than it does now?

We certainly had more of a selection among native North American game foods than we do now. Who eats partridge hens these days? Rabbit stew? Squab? Sounds barbaric, doesn't it? Just as chicken sounds barbaric to my vegetarian daughter.

There was a distinctly German flavor to food in the Twenties. Hard rolls were Kaiser rolls; cottage cheese was schmierkase; and we ate lots of hasenpfeffer and sauerbraten and fat German sausages.

Just remembering the food we ate for breakfast raises my cholesterol now: scrapple and hominy with applesauce; codfish cakes and mashed potatoes; waffles with ham or bacon – likewise pancakes or corn fritters with maple syrup; creamed chipped beef on toast or biscuits; corned beef hash on toast, topped with one or two poached eggs; kidney stew; steak and kidney pie; calves' liver and bacon; finnan haddie with potato cakes; fried eggs on top of potato cakes with applesauce; and, of course, four-minute boiled eggs with toast fingers.

We seldom had a glass of orange juice or even much fruit. Oscie occasionally prepared an orange on a fork for each of us. She peeled it with a very sharp knife, leaving not a trace of the bitter, white membrane. I can still feel the juice running down my arm and dripping from my elbow. Warning: Don't try this dish without a professional chef. Very labor-intensive. Very messy.

Although we went to Eastern Market for special cuts of meat – thick, beautiful pork chops or tender-as-butter calves' liver – my mother often phoned Mr. Javins at Center Market for game. He delivered venison steaks and rabbit and squab (baby pigeon), partridge, quail, guinea hen. If Brother or I were sick, we could count on having tiny squab on toast as a treat.

There was a stand at the wharf (I don't know which wharf; we just called it the wharf) that Mama used to call for delivery of blue crabs, lobster and oysters. There was not much shrimp – none in my childhood memory. Maybe in those days it didn't travel well from the warmer, shrimpier climates.

For just ordinary food, I can hear Granny on the phone with someone who ran a regular grocery store somewhere near Stanton Park, I think. (If we ran out of bread or milk or eggs, we could always "run down" to one of the little corner groceries a block or so away.)

"I'd like a pound of butter – your best butter," she would say. "A loaf of sliced Bond bread, two dozen of your freshest farm eggs, ten pounds of stone-ground white flour, ten pounds of white granulated sugar, and two quarts of cream-top milk. Be sure the milk has enough cream so that it isn't that blue, skim color. Five pounds of good beef for stew. Oh, and throw in a few bunches of parsley and a good-sized piece of ordinary beef liver. For the alligator."

The alligator would have been Blinky, a live alligator that our rather eccentric Aunt Mary had sent us from Florida. I don't know why Granny's explanation that the "ordinary beef liver" was for our weird pet of an alligator entitled her to free liver, but it did. Also, she expected – and got – free garnishes, like parsley, mint and other herbs.

Granny's everyday meals had to stretch to feed Granny and Grandpap, Granny's three sisters, an elderly maiden great-aunt or two or three, a female boarder, and whatever family members were in need of shelter at the moment. If this latter category included Shelton and his mother and grandmother, a porterhouse or large T-bone steak was added to the grocery order. For Shelton. A male.

Grandpap shared the lamb stew or meatloaf with the otherwise female household. Shelton, the twenty-some-year-old ne'er-do-well, required a large steak, to "keep up his strength."

At our apartment, one large steak fed all four of us every Thursday night, along with French fries and a salad. And maybe a pie from Sherrill's Bakery on Pennsylvania Avenue, S.E. Thursday was Oscie's night off and Mama cooked. Mama was a singer. On Sunday night we ate leftovers from the Sunday roast. The other nights of the week, Oscie proudly presented gourmet meals. Oscie had become a first-class cook. She would bring her triumphs to the table, then stand near the dining room door, arms folded over her chest, waiting until we had had a bite of each dish.

"How it taste?" she would ask, whether it was just the family or a dinner party of ten.

"Excellent, Oscie."

"You've outdone yourself with this oyster bisque."

"Best crown roast I've ever tasted."

She would quietly accept the accolades, then wave them aside with a swatting motion, as she turned toward the kitchen. "I knows *you* sick! ... Can't be that good."

Minutes later, she'd be back to hand around the platters for seconds, and accept more compliments. Or hand out some hard words to the guests.

"You want some more coffee?"

"I think I'll have just a wee bit more." This from a rather prissy great-aunt. "I shouldn't, but a little won't hurt."

"A little!" shrieked Oscie. "You already had two cups."

One winter night, the rector of St. Mark's and his friend, Mr. Beatty, were having dinner with us. "I know the weather report calls for snow," said Mr. Pettus, "but I doubt if we'll get any at all."

Oscie stopped passing around the mashed potatoes. "It won't snow? I knows *you* sick! Stick your head out the window." It was snowing a blizzard. Unoffended, Mr. Pettus and the other guests laughed heartily as Oscie enjoyed her small triumph.

As good as Oscie's food was, occasionally we sought out some special bakery or restaurant for something absolutely scrumptious.

Like pumpkin pie from Reeves's (that's what we always called it – Reeves's) downtown on F Street, N.W. Or, when my mother went downtown without me, she always brought home Reeves's matchless petits fours for me. Everyone else but Mama called them "petty fors." She pronounced them "p'tee foor," the French way. Of course. My mother was a singer.

Sometimes she and I would take the streetcar all the way out 14th Street, N.W., to Demonet's at Mount Pleasant, for pure cream vanilla ice cream and fresh raspberry sherbet. We did this in the summer – the season when people ate ice cream, in the Twenties. We would wait at the streetcar stop across East Capitol from the parlors until an open-air car came along. It was one way to cool off in the days before air conditioning.

It seems as if we did this ice cream adventure at least every week during every summer of my young life. But maybe we went just once. Whatever. It was memorable.

Oscie and I frequently went down to Sherrill's Bakery to bring back French apple cake or Charlotte Russe (lady fingers in a sort of cardboard cup of heavy whipped cream with a cherry on top).

No food experience in my very young life, however, comes close to my very first club sandwich, which I devoured at a big old fashioned hotel at Chesapeake Beach. I was about three years old, and we were on a rare family outing. We had traveled all the way to Chesapeake Beach by train which we boarded at a little station at Benning Road – I think it was. This was my first train trip. It took over an hour to get there.

And, at the beach, we rode in a canoe, an adventure which terrified me, and I screamed until Papa paddled us back to shore. But on shore, I had that fabulous club sandwich. That made it all right. I took it apart to eat it, because I couldn't fit it into my mouth.

Another unforgettable gourmet memory was formed closer to home. A neighborhood character who smelled (she didn't bathe) took me to tea in a restaurant somewhere down Independence Avenue, S.E., where the Rayburn House Office Building now stands. We went to The Ugly Duckling. I was about five years old, and I didn't want to be seen with her.

Despite my ungracious mood, the decor of the place delighted me: High-backed settles (benches) at each table, cobalt blue walls with bright yellow ducklings forming a lively border near the ceiling. My hostess ordered Cambric tea for me – half tea, half sweetened milk – and cinnamon toast.

I had had toast with a bit of butter and cinnamon sugar sprinkled on it before, but never cinnamon toast like this. Dripping butter, the toast was covered in layer on layer of sugar and cinnamon, then the whole thing crusted over in the broiler. I devoured the first dish. Then the second. And a third.

Many times since, I have tried to duplicate the cinnamon toast served at The Ugly Duckling, but, alas, the secret recipe probably lies buried somewhere beneath the garage of the Rayburn House Office Building. I can still taste that toast. And I can still smell Miss C.

CHAPTER 18

TIME OUT FROM CAPITOL HILL

Leonardtown entered my life when I was too small for my feet to reach the bare ground beneath the rope swing at the T. Lee Mattingly House. I could soar three or even four daring feet high by pushing against the back of an old hound dog named Jim, stretched out beneath me.

In those days, I couldn't say a soft J, so I called him Gim, which so delighted Papa that he made up a saying for me, using those sounds, and amusing everyone but me. It went:

Gim gumped up on the kildren's kest
and ate their kestnuts
and then went to kurse.

Jim came with the house. He didn't belong to us. Neither did the house. Thank heaven. It was a large wooden shack, located in the outskirts of Leonardtown, then a village in Southern Maryland, fifty-some miles from D.C. The main road looped around the ragged town green and led down the hill to a wharf on Breton Bay.

The house we were renting for a few weeks that summer was far on the other side of town from any water at all. Including inside plumbing.

The path to the smelly outhouse was lined with hollyhocks, whose beauty failed to make up for the inconvenience and the personal plumbing problems some of us developed in resistance to the two-seater.

And Mama never let Papa forget that his choice of a "summer retreat on Breton Bay" was far from the bay or a view of anything but neglected, overgrown fields in all directions.

At the end of summer, when we left the T. Lee Mattingly House for the drive home, we were looking forward to the flat over the parlors. Our "holiday quarters" had been that bad.

There didn't seem to be a chance that we would be traveling down to Leonardtown anytime soon again. But life is unpredictable. Especially if you have a friend like "Uncle Clem" Mattingly, the Leonardtown undertaker and chum of my father's.

It was Uncle Clem who had found us the T. Lee Mattingly disaster, but things had changed in the two or three years since that experience. First and foremost, my father had died. Maybe Uncle Clem was feeling protective toward the young widow whose family was in need of a summer refuge. This time she wanted a house with a view. Uncle Clem found us one – a gem. A big, solid, cream-colored clapboard, with open, pillared porches and screened porches and sleeping porches and even a kitchen porch, screened-in, across the back. It was known as the Bascom Broun house, for its builder. And now it was the Zurhorst house; Mama bought it.

Downhill beyond a well-grazed meadow, Breton Bay gently curved into the distance, all the way to the Chesapeake, and on a crystal-clear day, even showed us a sliver of Virginia.

On such days, Mama used to take pride in pointing out to guests a hazy gray something on the far horizon, and announcing with awe, "That's Virginia!" As if we could see the coast of West Africa from our front porch.

At the foot of the hill, where the Bay turned toward the Leonardtown wharf, was a buoy that marked the channel. Twice a week a genuine steamboat – straight out of the ante-bellum past – rounded that buoy, and sounded a few shrill notes on a whistle, announcing its arrival at the dock.

Actually, there were two steamboats that made the run from Washington: the plump side-wheeler Dorchester, and the longer, sleeker Northumberland, a sternwheeler. One came on Tuesday, the other on Thursday.

Early one May morning, with mist swirling over the waters of the Bay, our family was aboard the Dorchester as it rounded the bend.

As I was the youngest passenger, the bearded captain gave me the honor of sounding the landing whistle. (Brother got to give it an extra toot.)

Although Leonardtown was a convenient hour and a half drive from 301 East Capitol, my mother wanted us to arrive at our new summer home in gloriously outdated style. Mama was a romantic.

It was an overnight voyage from Washington.

Brother and I were allowed to stay up, and all night long we watched through the portholes as stevedores, bodies shining with sweat, unloaded crates of supplies at small, dimly lit docks along the Potomac and the Chesapeake.

They returned to the boat rolling hogsheads of sweet-smelling tobacco leaves bound for Washington and Baltimore. As their muscles strained to roll the barrels up the gangplank, the men sang, with a strong, muscular rhythm.

They were work songs, but at the same time gentle in the soft night air.

∽

The "Leonardtown house" up the hill from Breton Bay.

Three females at the Leonardtown house: Mamie Russell, Mama and me.

When the boat docked in the morning damp, we were the only passengers to get off. Uncle Clem was to meet us, but he wasn't there. It was just us: Mama, Granny, Brother, and I, seated on Grandma Zurhorst's steamer trunk, with a young lamb tethered to the handle, a caged parrot that kept repeating, "It looks like hell," a ginger kitten (my first personal pet, given to me by Mr. Gasch, an undertaker in Hyattsville, Maryland), and a spotted puppy with diarrhea. We left the alligator home.

Lacking cell phones, we had no way to contact Uncle Clem – except for Brother, who swore that he remembered the way up the hill to Uncle Clem's house, where we had visited before. He persuaded Mama to let him go.

In a half hour or so, here came a large black hearse racing down to the wharf, Brother with an "I told you I could do it" look of pride, and Uncle Clem at the wheel, face flushed, howling with laughter. "Aye de jeeminy craminies," he shrieked, "lived here all my life and never knew the boat come on Tuesday before." His left hand beat against the front door of the hearse with exuberance for this monumental lapse of memory. "One for the books! Aye de jeeminy craminies. That fool boat sure fooled me." And he loaded us all into the hearse.

He insisted that we have breakfast at his house. I could smell the food cooking as we opened the front door – potatoes boiling in a huge open pot, pounds of aromatic bacon sizzling in the biggest cast iron frying pan I'd ever seen, apples frying over low heat and releasing a tart, sweet aroma to complement the bacon, and large pans of home-made (of course) biscuits turning golden in the oven. A large bowl of brown eggs sat waiting to be fried.

Over all this delectable feast there arose a rich, creamy, meadowland scent of hand-churned butter – a much stronger, outdoors smell than packaged, city butter. Mixed in – and not unpleasantly – was the odor of kerosene used to fuel the stove. The steam from the boiling potatoes absorbed, blended and released all the aromas into the air together. Scrumptious.

Happily fed, we got packed into Uncle Clem's hearse again for the one-mile trip to the house on Foxwell's Road, up on a hill overlooking Breton Bay.

Mama – probably through Uncle Clem – had hired a house-keeper-cook, sight unseen, who was already ensconced in the house. It took a while for her to answer the door after Mama tapped on it. When the door finally opened, there stood a short, squarish woman of mahogany skin and half-closed eyes, barefoot, and clad only in a skinny pink chemise.

"Weegie?" asked my mother, with trepidation.

"Yes," she answered, in slurred, honeyed tones. "And who shall I say is calling?"

Weegie, who was clearly drunk, was holding the fort to protect it against intruders. "Are you expected?" she asked.

"Of course we're expected," said Mama. "We're expecting ... US! We own this house. Now please get some clothes on and let us in."

"Very well," said Weegie, amiably, as she shut and locked the door.

Eventually, Brother sneaked around to the back to get in the house. He opened the front door, quickly followed by Weegie, still barefoot and still in only the pink chemise, but with the addition of a wide-brimmed straw hat trimmed with a lavender ribbon. "Is this better?" she purred.

We trailed into the living room, leaving Uncle Clem to deal with the baby lamb, poll parrot, kitten, and puppy with diarrhea.

The situation had rattled us so much that nobody – not even Granny – knew what to do next. We were sort of milling about, leaderless, when a tall, erect, dark-skinned man walked into the living room with great dignity. "Just wanted to know if you needed anything, Ma'am," he said, addressing my mother.

"Who are you?" she asked him.

"I'm Son," he said, "Sonny Williams. Weegie's husband. We came as a pair. I guess you didn't know."

Mama stared blankly at him. Her jaw was dropping.

"Weegie's in our house out back, sleepin' it off. She be all right in a while. You had breakfast?"

"They've eaten at Mr. Clem's already," said a voice at the back end of the living room. It was Weegie, wobbly, but in control. She had put on a shapeless dress with an apron over it.

"Dinner will be at six o'clock," she announced.

"That's fine," said Mama, thoroughly intimidated.

Clearly, the dynamics of our household were changing. Hung over as she still was, Weegie was now in charge. Even Granny was outclassed. She was out of her realm so far from Capitol Hill. This was Weegie territory. Make no mistake about that.

With her eyelids lowered and her chin raised, Weegie's grammar shifted into the lofty third person. "Weegie will serve breakfast from 8 to 9." She went on to explain the rules of the kitchen and the hours it was closed.

She recommended that Mama establish a charge account at the grocery store on the town square – "before the day is out. They're expecting you."

Mama obediently agreed to go. As Weegie was leaving the room, Mama asked her to say again what her husband's name was – just to be sure.

"Son," she smiled. "I call him Son because that's what his mother called him," and she wavered almost gracefully toward her kitchen.

⌒∽

On our first weekend at the house, over Memorial Day, 26 uninvited guests arrived. With suitcases.

The majority of them were family and neighbors. It was as if Capitol Hill had packed up and moved to Leonardtown.

A mixed bag of ten or more invited guests were already embedded. Add 26 more and we filled every bed in the house, every sofa, easy chair, outdoor glider, and even the hammock, plus a few choice floor spots at the edges of the big, double living room.

We had but one bathroom.

Some of us that weekend slept four or five deep in a few double beds, including the old brass bed on the sleeping porch. That was usually Brother's, but because of the crowd, he was sharing it with three other teenaged boys, among them Ford Loker. Ford was a blond, lanky, lovable kid who was at least a head taller than the others and not yet used to the extra space his long arms and legs required.

It took a while for such a crowd to settle down, but eventually, the house fell silent, except for a few snorts and snores and the furtive flushing in the night.

Then with no warning the silence ended violently with a clang of metal – as if the Eiffel Tower had imploded on the sleeping porch.

For a long time nobody called out or ran to the scene. We all just lay there, wide awake, holding our breath as the clamor continued.

A few clunks, followed by a metal something hitting the bare floor of the porch, then slowly but noisily rolling down the floor's slight incline. And another and another, in a long succession.

Finally, when all had been quiet for a few seconds, the voice of Ford rent the air. "Aye gad!" he bellowed. "I done broke de bed."

He probably had pushed out a few brass rungs at the head of the bed, and then kicked out those at the foot. The bed didn't collapse all at once, but one rung at a time, with each brass piece rolling at its own pace down the slanted bare floor.

One of the sons of a distinguished judge ("de jedge") whose family had arrived in Southern Maryland with the earliest settlers, Ford chose to talk and act the role of hayseed. Mama was especially fond of him, and was pleased when he and Brother hit it off just a few days after we arrived in Leonardtown.

He knew everybody in town, of course, and Mama was eager to get acquainted.

"Ford, do you know Dr. Camalier?"

Ford hit his head and reeled backwards, as he shouted, "Know 'im? Aye gad, I raised 'im!" Dr. Camalier was old enough to be Ford's grandfather.

Ford never gossiped; he just passed along the facts. "Miss Bertie's out of the hospital. Brought her goiter home with her." He slapped his thigh like an old-timer. "Yep, got her goiter with her. Settin' right there on the mantelpiece in her living room, in a Ball jar. That's de Gawd's truth."

A year or so after we made Leonardtown our second home, Mama threw a dinner party for Ford's sister Susie who was leaving home to become a nun. Everything went smoothly – with Weegie cold sober – until dessert.

Something looked funny. Mama had told Weegie that she wanted apple pie à la mode, and she had ordered gallons of vanilla ice cream packed in dry ice to top it off. Gobs of white stuff adorned the pie. But what was it? Everybody was waiting politely for Mama to start, while heads bent lower and lower, peering into the dish, forks at the ready.

Finally Mama, who was a bit near-sighted, plunged in. And plunged right out again, making a face. That white stuff wasn't melting. It was heaps of mashed potatoes.

Furious, Mama tore into the kitchen in search of the ice cream – and of Weegie, who had celebrated a successful dinner, and was now, as she would put it, taking a well earned rest. In short, she was in her little house, out cold.

The kitchen porch off the back of our house was filled with a crew of men who were building a chicken coop for us, down near the barn. Each had a soup plate brimming with ice cream.

About two days later, when Weegie was beginning to recover, she was unfazed when Mama let her know how angry she was.

"Don't let it bother you, dear heart," Weegie cooed. "They wouldn't know the difference. And where that girl's goin', she'll be lucky if she ever sees an apple pie again. She won't be gettin' pie on the commode, that's for sure."

One dark night, Mama and I were out by the gate posts, examining the bricks Mama had dislodged that day on her first – and last – attempt to drive a car. As we looked at the damage, there was a rustling in the bushes by the road, followed by a muffled exclamation not meant for the ears of such as me, or Mama. She looked scared but held her ground.

"Who's there?"

Silence.

Then whispers between the men. In French.

Mama's face lit up. Even though I could barely see it in the distant glow of the porch light, I knew she was delighted. She spoke fluent French. And it flew off her lips as if she had been waiting for this moment.

Great guffaws filled the dark night as two men stepped out into the dim hint of light near the gate. They were smellier and grimier than any men I had ever been this close to. I was terrified of their blackened faces and ragged clothes.

"I'm gonna get Son," I announced, but before I could take off, Mama grabbed me and laughed, "No, Sissy, it's all right."

Then she turned toward the men and said, "You do speak English, don't you?" More laughter. "Come in."

A few minutes later, they were washed up – or at least the top dirt layer was off of hands and face – and one tall, skinny, dark-haired man (Brother Francis) and one heavy-set, Knute Rockne type, balding, with a permanent grin set into his generous face (Brother Theophane) were seated in our living room, each with a shot of Bourbon in hand.

They were members of the Roman Catholic Xaverian brotherhood from Camp Columbus, a Xaverian-run camp across the road (and up a steep hill) from us.

Mama had stumbled upon their hidden lair at the start of Smuggler's Week, a camp game which ran nonstop night and day for one full week – in the darkest phase of the moon.

These two had devised this rough game specifically for the boys of Camp Columbus – to "toughen them up," said Brother Theophane, and free them to do things their mothers would never let them do at home.

It divided the campers and brothers into smugglers and revenuers, with the revenuers tending to be the more gentlemanly of the group. Brothers Francis and Theophane, of course, were prime smugglers. There were echoes of the battles between real-life moonshiners and revenue officers of Prohibition, and of Al Capone gangsters tearing up the peace of Chicago. At the same time, the rough-housing never got violent.

That night at the gate was the beginning of a friendship like no other in our lives. Smugglers Week stretched into years of an extended family closeness that made our house and our family a kind of refuge, a comfort zone that many of the brothers sought out each summer.

Brother Francis and Brother Theophane held a special place, but there were also Brother Walter, Brother Herman – a mentor of Babe Herman Ruth whose name the young idol took as his own – among many others who thought of our house as home.

A familiar sight was Brother Francis, when Smugglers Week was over, seated at Mama's grand piano picking out an Irish tune with one finger, and singing, off-key, "Oura Mizzes McSalty had two pritty twins, faith, and two pritty divils they were. Hot dog ...." It went on for many verses.

Even more familiar was the sight of Mama at that keyboard giving her all to "Kathleen Mavoureen" or "I Met Her in the Garden Where the Praties Grow." And, of course, "Danny Boy."

Many of the brothers were Irish, and they used to sit listening and smiling as tears of remembrance filled their eyes.

As the years went on, the brothers brought priests, monsignors, a few bishops and other church dignitaries down to our house when they visited Camp Columbus. And Mama would sing their favorite songs for them.

There was usually another listener, perched on the arm of the rocker just outside the window next to the piano. A little jenny wren would sit there quietly, content to be in the audience.

One evening, as a member of the higher echelon of the Roman Catholic Archdiocese of Baltimore was leaving our house, he lingered at the door. "It's been so refreshing to be with Protestants," he said. "They don't confess to you. They sing to you."

Not everyone in Leonardtown was pleased at the close relationship between the Episcopalian Zurhorsts and the Roman Catholic brothers and their visitors. Leonardtown and its environs was about 99 percent Roman Catholic.

One summer day my mother had arranged to be driven up to Washington to do some shopping.

Brother Theophane heard about the trip and asked if he could bum a ride. For some reason, he wanted to be picked up at the Catholic high school in Leonardtown, instead of at the camp.

Many eyes were watching. Many tongues wagged. "I saw them with my own eyes. They were eloping. Brother Theophane and the widow Zurhorst. He got right in the car with her. I know they were eloping because Brother Theophane had a suitcase and he was wearing a hat."

That story took a long time to stop making the rounds.

The brothers were always welcome at our house. Except for the times the sisters from St. Cecilia's came, and then my brother – Snooie, or Brother – was stationed at the gate to keep them out.

Mama was angry with the male-centered Roman Catholic church for what she saw as its inexcusable neglect of the women in its care, the sisters and nuns. While the priests and brothers and men in holy orders in general were allowed informal clothes, some allowances and even vacations, the women were ignored, left to toil year round, and scrounge for their needs.

Short of inciting to riot, Mama did what she could to make their lives a tiny bit easier. Included in the package was a day trip now and then for the Holy Cross sisters from St. Cecilia's to the Leonardtown house, thanks to a small fleet of funeral cars.

I remember one especially hot day, when the humidity was high and there was no relief from any breeze. The sisters sat around on the porches, fanning themselves with palm fans from the parlors, iced tea and lemonade at their sides. They all chose spots to sit that offered a view of the bay; they had had only convent walls to look at for so long.

After a little while, Mother Prudenciana reached up and unhooked something at the back of her neck that allowed the huge, stiff – and stifling – collar to fall into her lap. Instantly, as if at a signal, the hands of all the other sisters did the same. A discreet little sigh escaped from a dozen or more throats.

Within the next few minutes, sleeves attached above the elbows with straight pins came off and were laid in a growing pile beside each rocker. Then the overskirts were lowered, stepped out of and added to the heap. Part of the veil was unattached. I stared, completely spellbound. To think that, at the convent school, it was a big deal to see a wisp of short hair escaping the bonnet. "Sister Benigna has brown hair!" Oh, to be the first to announce that great secret. Yet here they were, releasing secrets by the dozens – and still they were completely covered, but in fewer layers.

I was especially shocked to find that their heavy black habits were held together to such an extent by pins!

Well, at least their secrets were safe. No brothers – Xaverian or otherwise – entered the premises. The sisters went back refreshed, no matter the heat. And, under some reckoning, Mama might have earned herself an indulgence or so. Although I doubt it.

I had my own secret that I guarded, but Brotheophane, as we called him, found it out anyway. When I was nine or ten, occasionally a boy from Camp Columbus used to come down the hill and lie on the ground near me as I sat slowly turning but not swinging on the rope swing in our yard.

We didn't say much. Sometimes he would put a blade of grass to his lips and blow on it to make a sound. I'd laugh, and he'd grin. He always was dressed a little nicer than the other boys from camp, who often looked scruffy, with dirty knees. They never came anywhere near me, anyway. He was the only one. He usually wore knickerbockers, short britches that came just to the knee.

His name was Phil Ryan, and he was from Philadelphia. I thought he was very handsome. Although I can't remember his features, I can still hear the sound of his voice and his gentle laugh. He always made me feel that he and I shared a secret. But he never talked about any secrets between us. He was just there. Sweet, gentle, manly.

There was another boy in Leonardtown that Brother used to tease me about, and I disliked him. Soon Brother's friends picked up on the taunts: "Sissy's got a boyfriend, Sissy's got a boyfriend," they'd chant. "Danny, Danny, Dandy."

They did it one evening when Brotheophane was over, and with a wink at me, he said, "Sissy's got a boyfriend. But I don't think she'd say it was Danny." He lifted a quizzical eyebrow. "It's the Ryan boy, isn't it?"

"NO!" I cried out, and ran from the room. At that moment, I was furious with Brotheophane. The Ryan boy wasn't my boyfriend! Or even a friend. He was just somebody who came down the hill when I happened to be in the yard. That's all.

If he hears that I'm bragging that he's my boyfriend, he'll get scared off and never come again, I worried.

Auntie (she pronounced it Ahntie) Taylor, a snobbish friend of the family, was in the living room when this discussion was taking place. I had found a hiding place in the hall. From there, I could hear but couldn't be seen.

"Where is this Ryan boy from?" she asked Brotheophane.

"Philadelphia," he said.

"Well, well," she commented, loading each word with meaning. "Is there any chance that this young swain who's calling on this child [she never called me anything but "this child"] could be a member of the Thomas Fortune Ryan family? If so, she's made quite a catch. Quite a catch, indeed. Philadelphia aristocracy, the Thomas Fortune Ryans. And old money. This is a match to be encouraged."

By now the Ryan boy's occasional saunters down the hill had been blown all out of proportion. I was humiliated. To avoid seeing him again, I stayed in the house and away from the swing.

It was August, drawing near to camp's closing time, and he had stopped coming. I was sure it was because of what he must be thinking I had said. I was miserable.

I was sitting at the big, round kitchen table watching Weegie make Maryland beaten biscuits one day, when Son come in the room with a big, sly grin on his face. "Miss Sissy," he said, "you have a gentleman caller. Says he came to say goodbye."

Weegie, who was keenly aware of everything that was going on within a radius of at least five miles, wiped the sweat off her forehead with her apron and warned Son: "If this is one of Mr. Snooie's jokes, I'll make you sorry you ever ..."

"No," said Son. "I swear to God. I'm not lyin'. There's a young man from the camp waitin' to see Miss Sissy. That's the truth."

I went to the front door, holding my breath. He was standing there. The Ryan boy. He put out his hand, tentatively, as if he wasn't sure if I would take it. We had never touched before.

"I came to say goodbye," he said.

I took his hand. But did I smile? Did I say anything?

I just remember going back to the kitchen after he left and saying, in a while, "He came to say goodbye ... to me."

At least 50 years later, I met a charming woman who mentioned the Xaverian brothers. I said I had known several when we had a summer home near a camp that they ran.

"Camp Columbus?" she asked. "My late husband went there. I don't suppose there's a chance that you knew him. His name was Phil Ryan."

On that day when I nearly drowned – or choked to death on the green muck – I was sitting in the beached rowboat, the one with a hole in the side, when Brother and three or four of his chums came down the hill to the beach.

Our house was up the dirt road that led down to Foxwell's Point, a flat jut of land where the Foxwells lived in their comfortable country house at the water's edge.

I was allowed to go down there alone because I'd promised not to go in the water or even out on the short dock where groups of us sometimes went crabbing with bait on a string and a net. I was a safe, unadventurous kid of eight or so.

A few trees grew right down to the water, shading the narrow strip of sandy beach, and putting me in the shadows. Brother and his crew didn't know I was there – at first.

About thirty feet offshore was what Brother dramatically called "The Old Sunken Vessel," a shipwreck partially under water, its deck covered with green slime. The slippery planks jutted high above the waterline at the bow, and sank sharply into the muck in the submerged stern.

Brotheophane and Mama and Granny and Weegie and Son and everybody with any sense sternly warned us not to go near the old wreck. I took their admonitions seriously, of course.

Brother's eyes sparkled with the thrill of just thinking about going aboard.

As the group neared my unintentional hiding spot, Brother was explaining that this was the "perfect time to do it." There were always three or four seaworthy rowboats tied to one of the tree trunks or a low branch. I don't know who owned them. A pair of oars had been thrown onto higher ground. "See," Brother called out, "we've got everything we need. This is the perfect time to board her. And nobody'll ever know."

He was making them swear never to tell, when our cousin Robert, close to Brother's age, jerked a thumb in my direction. "What about her?" he groaned, as he spotted me.

A massive moan escaped from the throat of every conspirator. "Cripes," one whined. "This ruins everything." They argued among themselves, trying to agree on ways to keep me quiet.

I cringed down into the bottom of my rotten boat, saying nothing, because I knew that I couldn't *not* tell Mama. Brother called me "Tattletale" for good reason.

Suddenly, he came up with what he saw as the perfect solution: They'd take me with them. His reasoning was that if I boarded with them I couldn't tell on them because I would be as guilty as they were, and, to protect myself, I'd keep quiet.

Which showed that he didn't understand the modus operandi of a tattletale: You tell no matter what.

The boys piled into one of the rowboats, and I didn't move. Brother kept telling me to come on, and when I didn't, he pulled out the trump card – the old "I'll give you three" threat. He knew it always worked on me.

I stayed put; he started counting: "Onnnnnnnnnne ... twooooooooooo ... thuuuuuuuurrrrrrrrrrrrrrr ...."

Terrified, I got into the rowboat. What could have been a more ominous threat than drowning in the hold of this old boat, choking on putrid, green slime?

Yet such was the fear of Brother's getting to the end of "thrrrrrrrreeeeeee" that I surrendered. Invariably.

The boys rowed out to the sunken hull, and one by one, they climbed over the side, leaving my brother and me in the rowboat. He gave me a final shove as I wailed loudly.

One of my Mary Janes touched the foul deck, and SLURP, over I went on my belly in slippery silence straight down into the black watery darkness of the hold, my mouth and nose filling with green slime and brackish water.

The next thing I remember was Brother's hand grabbing my dress and pulling me to the splintery planks of the upper deck far above the waterline. As I coughed and spat out the ooze, I saw faces looking down at me, wide-eyed with fear. I knew even then that their fear was more for the punishment they'd get than for my condition.

The reception the boys received was not gentle. But Brother, as usual, emerged – at least in his eyes – as a hero.

"I saved her life," he bragged to anyone who would listen. And to my disgust, there were several who listened. And admired his bravery.

Cheeeeez.

We were grounded (me, too!) after that fiasco – "You'll have to learn to stand up to him, Sissy." We couldn't leave the house for a few days, and we were deep into a mid-summer hot spell. No air conditioning. Or even electric fans.

Then it rained, and the humidity levels rose.

We played board games until we were throwing tiles and cubes and fake money at each other. The house seemed ready to burst with the pent-up energy of banister-sliding, leap-frogging, wrestling, pre-teen males. Finally, Mama took Brother aside, said something to him, and he emerged with that "Eureka!" look, yelling as if he had just been struck with a brilliant idea.

"Know what let's do?" he asked, with excitement. "Let's watch movies!"

First-time visitors cheered. "What have you got? Tom Mix?" "Hoot Gibson?" "How about Buster Keaton?"

"You'll see," Brother promised, casting threatening looks at the whining and wiggling regular visitors who knew what was coming. He led us into the long, skinny bedroom that previous owners had sliced off the side of a large room at the back of the house.

The cramped quarters soon filled with what seemed like hordes of unwashed boys, reeking of sweat, their sockless feet putrid in rubber-soled sneakers.

Brother threaded the film into the projector, obviously unsure of the procedure but receiving much advice from several boys who knew even less about doing it than he did. Windows were closed, the door shut tight to keep out the light. Also the air.

Soon the light from the projector was sputtering against one wall, with the sprocket wheel going clickety clack.

"Is it Douglas Fairbanks?" asked a hopeful voice in the audience. "Nah, it's a Western," offered another.

Then in shaky letters the title appeared on the wall: THE VENUS FLY TRAP. This was followed by a lily-like flower (in black and white, of course) that seemed to linger projected forever. Probably thirty seconds.

Then action! A fly buzzed in from the side of the picture and landed on the flower. We all leaned toward the image, sweat dripping from the tips of our noses.

The fly circled the rim of the petal, over and over, each time going down lower into the flower. We all held our breath. Danger lurked within the white folds of that deceptively benign flower. And then a soundless SNAP (we could hear it) as the Venus Fly Trap closed tight shut and swallowed the fly. A few gasped.

"THE END" flashed on the screening wall. Somebody in that stifling, crowded room flipped on the light. Another one turned off the projector to stop the end of the reel from flapping against the machine. Everyone made for the door.

The boys loudly announced that they'd been gypped. "You said it was a movie! That stupid thing was no movie. Don't you have no Wild West shows?"

As a defense, Brother claimed he had never seen the short film before, that it had come with the projector. Maybe he was telling the truth, but nobody believed him.

Actually, we played The Venus Fly Trap a lot of times. Things got that dull. When it rained.

⁂

At the front end of the long, double living room was a strange, boxy chair that we identified with Auntie Taylor forever after the incident with the mouse. She was seated in that chair at the time.

Auntie Taylor was a buxom lady who wore a lorgnette on a long, silver chain, which she clutched to her bosom with her left hand while she peered through the fancy spectacles in her right hand.

Bits and pieces of her ample chest sometimes had to be tucked back in when they overflowed, as they often did.

She was a friend of my mother's, although she was nearer Granny's age. The widow of the captain of a luxury liner, she had traveled extensively, and frequently dropped foreign words and phrases into her conversation.

In fact, she was in the middle of a tale about "dear Firenze" when she suddenly stopped and reached for her lorgnette. As she leaned far forward, with more and more frontage escaping, she let out a whoop at the sight of a mouse sitting boldly upright on its haunches near her feet.

Unperturbed, the little creature got down on all fours and slowly – and very un-mouselike – made its way around the room, paying sociable visits to one and all.

Somebody called out, "Look, it's bleeding."

But the trail it was leaving wasn't blood; it was purple juice from the blackberries that Granny was fermenting in the kitchen pantry to make wine.

The mouse was drunk.

And what of the chair where Auntie Taylor was sitting? With its Gothic carvings and solid base, it looked rather ecclesiastical. *Au contraire*, as Auntie Taylor would say.

Its boxy bottom was built for the Prohibition years. The front panel had a concealed lock. Inside stood several Mason jars of bootleg whiskey straight from the still of a St. Mary's County sheriff, plus some of last year's home-made blackberry wine.

The mouse had sampled this year's wine before its time.

Once a year, Leonardtown, like "Brigadoon," awoke from its drowsy, restful state and came wide awake every night for a full week in mid-summer when the James Adams Floating Theater tied up at the town wharf.

This was the same riverboat that Edna Ferber lived on for a while one summer when she was writing – what else? – "Showboat," of course.

From the town and miles around, St. Mary's County folks filled the creaky seats of the theater every night of its stay, thrilling to the dances and dramas – no, not melodramas – presented on the unpretentious stage. The plays were usually sort of folk art theater. Nothing violent, nor vulgar, nor innovative. Just wonderful, low-keyed entertainment, always with a villain and a love interest.

The James Adams Floating Theater was as plain as an old covered barge. It bore no resemblance outwardly to the increasingly ornate showboats made for the movies in years to come. But we knew the origin of that history-making and social mores-breaking drama, and took a special pride in our intimate connection. We had been where the idea of "Showboat" had been born, and loved it for the rest of our lives.

The date of its last appearance in Leonardtown was 1940.

Looking back on our house near Leonardtown, I often see Mamie leaning against the big elm tree in the middle of the circle formed by the driveway. I can even hear her moaning.

Mamie Russell was her name, and she had begun to expand around the waist. We thought she was pregnant. We even named the baby – I wanted to call it Lindy after Lindbergh, and Brother wanted Babe for Babe Ruth. The name became just another excuse for bickering between us.

Mama asked Son if he thought this peculiar behavior of leaning against the tree and moaning was normal if Mamie was pregnant.

Son was wearing his battered old black felt hat. When Mama asked the question, he took off the hat and held it in front of his face. He didn't want Mama to see him laughing. But I could see him shake.

"You think Mamie's pregnant, Miss Edwinetta? How you think she got that way?"

Mama, whose knowledge of horses (I did explain that Mamie Russell was a horse, didn't I?) was limited to the old nag that belonged to Tom the huckster from A Street, looked embarrassed and said, "Well, the uh, the usual way."

Son shook his head. "Ain't another horse, male or female, within two, three miles of here. Anyway Mamie's twenty-four years old." He scratched his short-cropped head. "If you ask me, I

159

think she's got the green apple colic. Gives 'em gas, and makes 'em swell up like that."

Son knew some man down near Piney Point. "He can fix horses real good." So he sent out word along the back-road grapevine, and in a day or so – when Mamie looked as if she was going to burst – the man drove into the yard, rattling away in a dust-covered old Model T.

As a goodly number of us stood and watched, expecting to see him give Mamie a pill or a swig from some medicine bottle, the man deftly inserted a thin-bladed knife into Mamie's belly. A gush of wind loudly escaped from Mamie at the same time as shocked gasps burst forth from the crowd. Some ran from the scene.

The amateur vet massaged Mamie's shrinking belly, as she visibly relaxed. Mamie turned her head toward him, and, I swear, gave him a look of gratitude.

She was good for a few years after her colic. Mama found an old, used buggy to hitch Mamie to, and although this ex-racer had been intended as a riding horse for Brother, she took well to the buggy, too.

To return to the Leonardtown house in my mind's eye, I view it from the squeaky, smelly leather seat of the old buggy as it crests the hill leading down past the house to Foxwell's Point on the bay. We stir up a cloud of dust as we go.

Sometimes Brother, sometimes Son, is beside me, holding the reins that are draped over Mamie Russell's broad back. Her ears stand erect and still. Her coarse-haired black tail seems poised, ready to flick off the fly or two always gathered there.

Down at the end of the road, beyond our house and the green meadow between, is Breton Bay, curving and weaving its way in and out of green spits of land, flowing into the wide Potomac, and then all the way to the BIG bay – the Chesapeake – in the far distance. We often rented a boat to go on those waters.

Some of that land is humanized with a lone house here and there, and sometimes a gray-planked tobacco barn, with the long leaves airing in the rafters.

As we round a curve, I can hear Jim Blakistone shouting above the loud sputtering of the motorboat's gasoline engine, "That's Paw Paw 'Holla' over t' starb'rd. Good rock fishin' there when the weather's right."

We hired Jim to take us down the bay fishing several times a summer. A map of those parts comes alive with Jim's voice. "Can you feel the change of air? We're comin' into the Potomac. Colton's Point comin' up yonder," and he points toward a tree-shaded grassy shore. "Bushwood Landing just ahead. Good tobacco land in these parts." We are up the Wicomico River now.

The sound of his voice lingers like the memory of the iridescent pools floating in the bilges that sloshed under a wooden trap door in the bottom of the boat. And smelled ominously of gasoline.

We sat on a ledge around the perimeter of the old fishing boat, protected by a canvas awning.

We seldom went as far as the Chesapeake in Jim's boat, as I recall. But we did come within the distant view of a hazy shore that Mama loved to point out as "Virginia, over there."

Weegie packed scrumptious lunches for us to take with us. When we were finished, we dumped the leftovers and the paper bags overboard.

Before the judgment call on that 1920's breach of environmental manners, we must leave the boat for a moment and return to the buggy. Mamie is showing her stubborn streak again. She's pulling her old trick of standing stock still, refusing to budge if she can't have her way. What she doesn't understand is that this moment is all in my head, a figment of my memory.

We can't go through those gates, Mamie. We don't live there anymore. We've just conjured up a few minutes from the past – shifted into real time, where all things are NOW.

But since we're here, maybe I can get in the house and out again before they know I'm here. Just long enough to run through The Venus Fly Trap once more. There's always hope that this time the fly will escape, fly away before the trap snaps shut.

It's worth a try.

And if this attempt fails, that's okay too. The motorboat, and Paw Paw Hollow, and Mamie Russell, and Brother Theophane and Sister Prudenciana, and Brother and Mama and Weegie and Son and pie on the commode – they're all still there. Like time waves or radio waves we can tune in on once we get the hang of it.

Even the Ryan boy is there. Oh, especially the Ryan boy. He will come to say good-bye throughout eternity.

And those two men on the bay side porch ... Isn't that Brotheophane and Brother Francis? Where are the rockers? The house looks so empty.

"We had to go down there as soon as we heard," Brotheophane told me. "Frank and I drove straight from Baltimore. The camp was closed for the winter, of course, but we had to be at the house ....

"We just stood there on the empty porch, and remembered her ...

"And wept."

(Brother Theophane told me this a few months after Mama's death.)

CHAPTER 19

THE SCHROEDERS

Every couple of weeks, Mama and I would take the streetcar down Pennsylvania Avenue, S.E., to go to my Grandfather Schroeder's family homestead at 524 Ninth Street for a visit.

We got off at the ancient U.S. Naval Hospital at Ninth and Pennsylvania. In my mind it was identified with the Civil War era illustrations in old books – especially Louisa May Alcott's *Little Women*, or maybe *Jo's Boys*. Indeed, it had been built in 1866 to serve wounded veterans of the Civil War, although we knew it in its later incarnation as an "Old Sailors' Home."

Further incarnations followed, with eventual transfer to the D.C. government, which let the property go to seed. For decades, it stood its ground, hoary, ungroomed, almost derelict, but refusing to give up the ghost. And now the Old Naval Hospital has won the battle. As of this writing, thanks to a determined band of neighborhood volunteers, it is being reborn as the Hill Center.

We never went through the gates into the rough grounds, but I wanted to.

To me it was a kind of gateway to the past, the entrance to a very special and old part of Capitol Hill. My mother made sure that Brother and I were familiar with these neighborhood treasures: the Marine Barracks, down Ninth at G, and a few blocks farther south, on the river, the Navy Yard.

At the Marine Barracks, facing G Street, is the Commandant's House, a white brick colonial home of great dignity and authority. This is the oldest public building in continuous use in a city filled with historic structures. It's also one of the most human of public buildings. A beauty.

In summer, the deeply moving Evening Parade is held on the Parade Grounds that form the center of the Marine Barracks, the oldest active post of the Marine Corps.

It's a ceremony like no other in this city: superbly played band music that taps into a well of patriotism that you hadn't known was there, deep within you. Precision drills that stir the soul (what is it about the metallic thwack of many rifles hitting many palms at the exact same instant that is so riveting?). War-torn battle flags moving like ghosts in the night.

Then, in a grand finale, the massed battalion marches off the field – usually to a Sousa beat – and leaves it in silent darkness. But only for a breath-holding moment.

A spotlight finds the scarlet tunic of a lone bugler on the ramparts above the barracks. The audience of several thousand keeps utter silence as the bugler sounds taps ... a silence that often lasts until long after the final note fades into the thin night air.

A few short blocks down G Street from the Marine Barracks is John Philip Sousa's birthplace, at 636 G. (He was born there in 1854.) The former Sousa home is not open to the public, but it is a thrill to see it, especially after hearing so much of his music at the Evening Parade.

The "March King" moved many times within D.C. As a boy, he used to claim that he lived "on the Navy Yard." He didn't, but he says in his autobiography, *Marching Along*, that the boys who did live in the close-in neighborhood of "the Yard" were tough, gun-toting critters who were at home on the Potomac or the Anacostia, fishing, or quail shooting "across the Bennings Bridge and into Prince George County."

The scrappy young Sousa clearly identified with this element. With a gang mentality, the "in boys" divided familiar parts of the city into regions: There was the Navy Yard, Capitol Hill, Swampoodle (near the now Union Station) and the island, which was south of Pennsylvania Avenue, between Tiber Creek and the Potomac. All this according to Sousa.

Today public access to the Navy Yard has become limited, but I will always remember the childhood thrill of going to the foot of Eighth Street and walking through that stately Latrobe Gate (an arched opening in a vast white wall that is a proper ceremonial entranceway), and emerging into one of the loveliest – and small-est – parade grounds for miles around.

George Washington personally endorsed Benjamin Stoddert's choice of the Navy Yard site. In 1799 it was a "stark and bare wilderness."

Even now, its late 18th century charm still radiates from the long rows of attached houses, each pure white, graced by colonial porches on the second floor. These officers' quarters face the parade grounds and form part of the wall.

It's a very gentle looking military installation, but its history is as violent as any spot in Washington.

In 1814, during the War of 1812, British troops were approaching the city, some of them by way of the Potomac River. The Navy

Yard was a prime target. That's where the nation's fleet was being built and maintained. And where the British hoped to repair their own ships.

The Yard's Commandant, Capt. Thomas Tingey, was also a prime target. He was British-born, with a price on his head.

President James Madison and most of his Cabinet gathered near the Navy Yard to decide what to do. The decision was to "Fire the Yard." Soon the Navy Yard was in flames, as was much of the city.

Capt. Tingey sadly carried out orders, and fled to Virginia in a small boat.

British forces found smoldering ruins. Still standing was the massive wall, penetrated by the Latrobe Gate (the same Latrobe who designed the first Capitol dome), the guardhouse, Commandant's house, and a few officers' quarters, plus the Commandant's office, facing the river.

These buildings are still there, relics of a turbulent era, still attractive against the later factories and arsenals.

Legend has it that the ghost of Capt. Tingey even now appears in a second-floor window of the beautiful house of the Commandant, spy glass pointed down the river, anxiously on guard against the return of the British.

The Captain is certainly not peering at visitors who have come to stroll around the Navy Yard on the banks of the Anacostia River, or explore the excellent museums on the grounds. The public can now enter these old precincts only with special passes or when in tour groups, with reservations.

Martial music – mostly Sousa – still drifts out of the Navy History Center on the Parade Ground.

In its earliest days as a major shipyard, fife and drum music enlivened the scene along the river.

And back before the needs of a nation's defense took over this choice land where two rivers meet, perhaps swarthy lads in buckskin knelt at the water's edge, hollowing out logs to make canoes. Canoes that could, perhaps, glide down this river into ever wider and deeper waters until they reached a sea as big as the noonday sky.

It was such a sea that Christian Schroeder set sail on in 1840, with his wife, Dorathea, and four-year-old son, Augustus Wilhelm. They were leaving the homeland of Hanover (now part of Germany) to come to America. The same Hanover that the Zurhorsts had left a few generations earlier.

After a three-month voyage, they landed at Baltimore, and went first to a farm at Four Corners, on Colesville Road in Montgomery County, Maryland (less than a ten-minute drive from my present home). They soon rented a house a few blocks from the Marine Barracks, and the family lived in the area from 1840 until the house at 524 Ninth St. was built in 1856. That was two years after Christian died "of disease contracted in line of duty."

He had enlisted in the U.S. Marine Band in 1840, and served close to four enlistments of four years each, before his death in 1854.

He is buried in historic Congressional Cemetery, as is most of the family.

Christian's widow, Dorathea, lived on until 1884, not speaking a word of English until a few weeks before her death, when she spoke nothing but English – without an accent.

Their only child, Augustus (later cut to August) Wilhelm Schroeder, had been a trained musician from boyhood, no doubt learning first from his father, a military bandsman when back in Hanover. August's primary instrument was the cornet, although he played several instruments.

He played in a few bands as a very young man, and when he turned 21, he enlisted in the U.S. Marine Band, and remained a member for the next 19 years.

He formed Schroeder's Orchestra in 1878. After 40 years of infusing the city with the sounds of music – band music, ballroom music, chamber music, wedding music, funeral music, ragtime music, whatever the occasion called for – August Schroeder died on June 25, 1918. He was 82 years old.

The family that Mama and I visited at the Schroeder household in the Twenties was much livelier than the people at Granny's on A Street. Younger, too, relatively speaking. Plus (big difference) there were great-uncles among the great-aunts at 524 Ninth. And always a fresh-baked cake.

Our visits varied with the seasons.

From spring into early fall, I couldn't wait to jump onto the two-seated wooden glider in the side yard. That long strip of grass and a swing to ride in seemed like heaven after the cold bricks and cement of 301 East Capitol. There had been a similar glider there when Mama was a girl. We have pictures of her on it.

The Schroeder house was one of the few on Ninth Street with a side yard (narrow, but green, and now filled with a narrow house, alas).

In my memory there is always a fruit tree in bloom or bearing fruit. A peach tree? Let's say that's what it was: a peach tree. And throughout August there was always at least one peach within reach of the glider, dripping sticky juice.

We went home loaded with peaches that we shared with the men downstairs and Mr. Pettus and Mr. Beatty, around on Third Street.

There was also a cherry tree at 524 Ninth. It was dotted with wine-dark, plump cherries in early summer. Then toward the back of the yard, a squatty, arthritic tree bearing small, ugly little apples too tart to eat raw, but perfect for pies.

One day we arrived just as Jeff, the handyman, was mowing the lawn. He was singing. The hand mower made clicking sounds as it sliced into the grass, leaving it rough but fresh and sweet-smelling. A bit like the fragrance of newly washed sheets drying in the sun.

Some of the Ninth Street homes had tiny front yards too small to mow, so they were planted in bushes. They still are.

A winter visit was a different matter altogether. We would go up the brick side path, to the door in the middle of the house, bypassing the front door that led from the porch. The house was (is) not much wider than about twelve feet across, but deep.

A left turn from the side door took us to the vast kitchen, where I invariably asked for a drink of water just to use the enamel dipper hanging by the pump at the sink. There was a well; no piped running water. I wished we had had a well at home.

At the far back of the kitchen was a door that led to an attached and enclosed outhouse. I never used that inconvenience because it was so cold in winter. It didn't smell. (But then, how would I know? I never used it. I just know it didn't smell.)

A right turn as we entered the house led into a small dining room. Or was it just a back parlor? (Where was the dining room? I think I've lost the dining room.)

Whatever it was, it was dominated by a massive sideboard, heavily carved with heads of eagles and foxes and wolves and acorns and pine boughs and all manner of wondrous things that I found absolutely awesome.

Masterpiece though it was, I was constantly in fear that I might inherit it.

"Someday it'll be yours," Aunt Leila used to say.

I'd cringe.

Where would I put it?

This family heirloom that dwarfed all else in the tiny house had been hand-carved by an American Plains Indian, probably Sioux, who was recuperating in the Schroeder home after an illness. He was an Episcopal clergyman.

I never inherited the magnificent piece. Thank God.

In the front parlor were the Schroeder "family jewels" – an upright piano kept in perfect pitch, all manner of musical instruments leaning against the walls and furniture, slim chairs paired with music stands holding sheet music, and, it seemed to me, every other inch of floor space holding a forest of pedestals bearing heads and busts of the world's greatest composers.

That room was a booby trap for a small child. One false step . . .

"Watch, dear. Don't get too close." From Aunt Emmie.

"Don't run among the busts, darling. They were Papa's most prized possessions. Aside from the instruments, of course." Aunt Rita fluttered a handkerchief over the rakish beret of Richard Wagner, looking pleased with himself from a pedestal by her side.

*A gathering at the Schroeder house on Ninth Street. Young
Edwinetta is second from left in front. Granny and Grandpap
are in the second row on the right.*

Grandpap and Mama in the side yard at the Ninth Street house.

Edwinetta, the adored, only Schroeder granddaughter.

*The revered "Four Generations" picture. Seated: August Wilhelm
Schroeder with Charles Stewart Zurhorst, Jr. on his lap. Standing: John
Christian Schroeder and Edwinetta Schroeder Zurhorst.*

Aunt Leila took special pride in a violin locked in its case across the room. "That one is priceless," she whispered, as if afraid to disturb it. "Absolutely priceless. Only Uncle Raymond may touch that one."

Uncle Raymond was the indisputable First Violinist of this family of fine musicians. I often heard tales of the praise given him by the noted violinist Eugène Ysaÿe.

I tended to dismiss such promotion of clan members. How could they be so illustrious if they were in *our* family?

One overwhelming presence in that little room put all others – living and dead – in perspective: the untamed, uncombed, leonine head of Ludwig von Beethoven. It was he who ruled over the gods of this musical pantheon from atop the upright piano. His thick brows scowling *out loud*, he took charge of the small gathering of greatness as the unquestioned master.

In this household, Beethoven occupied the same place of honor as did the Madonna on the wall of the Tappan's living room on A Street, across from Granny's.

I was too young to recognize most of the musical luminaries placed throughout the room, but everyone in that household felt it a personal responsibility to reacquaint me with each head on every visit.

And I wouldn't have recognized his music when I heard it at that early age, but I do recall worrying a bit about Franz Liszt. I thought he looked pale and sickly. Maybe somebody should make him get a haircut. Or take his temperature.

This has just come to me. I don't think there was a bust of Mozart in that room.

No Mozart?

Maybe I just didn't know him when I saw him. Because you'd think ... wouldn't you?

I didn't see this packed little room until the 1920s, so I missed out on its most vital years – from the 1860s, on past the turn of the 20th century. August no doubt mastered several instruments here, and passed on his musical knowledge and ability to his sons. Here he practiced triple-tongue passages on his cornet, demanded flawless bowing on cello and violin, the highest standards of technique and emotion combined on the piano keyboard – and when he himself had conquered several instruments and shaped the musical ears and hands of his sons, he turned to mastering orchestral scores and conducting them. Then he handed on that art, too.

Here, August warmed his feet on the fender of the Latrobe stove in the front parlor after long parades in the cold – most likely down Pennsylvania Avenue.

In this room his lovely Altazera (nee Henderson of Green Springs, Virginia) served hot chocolate and five-layered caramel cake to her husband and perhaps his fellow Marine Band musician and friend, Antonio Sousa. The father of John Philip.

Often other bandsmen stopped by after a debutante ball or a concert at the White House. Did they talk of the troubled Mr. Lincoln wrestling with his loneliness? Or his sadness at the death of a son? Was he embarrassed over Mrs. Lincoln's strange behavior? Or had he requested – once again – that the band play his favorite "Dixie"?

Who was home that night – that unspeakable night – when the pounding of hoof beats woke the neighborhood around Eleventh Street and all approaches to the old wooden bridge across the Anacostia? Men on horseback were headed for southern Maryland in pursuit of suspects in the shooting of the President. The posse grew as they neared the bridge.

My oldest great-aunts and -uncles often told me that they remembered the clamor and the shouts from the streets, waking them that night. "The President's been shot," they remembered hearing, and they were frightened. People took to the streets for more news.

My grandfather, the eldest child, would have been about five years old at the time of the assassination. A realist, Grandpap always took pains to keep the story straight, explaining that he couldn't swear that he had actually *heard* John Wilkes Booth and his pursuers racing down Eleventh Street, two blocks away, but he had heard the *story* so many times that he almost believed it himself. It kept growing in the telling, he said, until all of the Schroeder children had taken part in the historic event, whereas in 1865 only two of the ultimately twelve children had yet arrived.

Where did they all sleep, these dozen children, mother and father, plus paternal grandmother, a few occasional relatives from the homeland, and a Sioux master wood carver Episcopal minister? There were only three bedrooms in the 524 Ninth Street house, all reached by an enclosed, twisted stairway tucked into the back parlor wall like an elongated coat closet.

The master bedroom, off of a tiny landing at the top of the steps, could hardly have been bigger than ten feet square; the other two rooms – the back one approached through the front one – accounted for the only other sleeping space. And no bathroom, even up to the 1950s. Yet they were the cleanest people I knew.

Of course, every bed had its chamber pot and its water pitcher and basin for ordinary use. But what about the emergencies that needed instant clean up – especially in a family of so many children? Clarence gets diarrhea, Susie throws up, Raymond wets the bed, Leila gets her first period. Robert spills the goose grease, Rita breaks a mirror and gets a deep, bleeding cut.

The clean-up water must come from the pump in the kitchen, and needs to be heated. It must be warmed on the stove – provided someone has remembered to keep the fire going – and carried upstairs in a kettle.

Did they have mass baths by the kitchen stove on Saturday nights? Two shifts – one for the girls, one for the boys? Fortunately, the 12 were evenly gender-divided, a stroke of fortune that made sleeping and bathing a bit simpler.

With no central heating, houses were cold in the wintertime, so clothing was heavy, and of wool, usually, for its warmth. And it was often scratchy and uncomfortable. If it kept you warm, it could also make you sweat. (To be delicate, it used to be said that horses sweat, men perspire and ladies bloom.) It definitely made you itch, this rough weave.

Tissues hadn't been developed yet and colds required mounds of handkerchiefs. All of which had to be washed – or boiled in a huge pot, next to the pot of diapers that were kept boiling every day for countless years in the Schroeder household, where there seemed to be a never-ending supply of newborns to take the place of every one potty- trained.

When emergency water was needed in a second-floor bedroom, what did they do with the gallons of used water? Throw it out the window?

As for the under-the-bed "slop jars," they were carried down the stairs, every morning, through the dining room and kitchen, to the outhouse at the back of the kitchen. Always covered, of course.

So, for all but a privileged few, there was little time for leisure, yet a surprising number of people in those days seemed to find time to have fun from simple pleasures. Maybe because there *was* so little time.

Bringing pleasure to the people was what August Schroeder's life in the United States Marine Band was all about. Pleasure ... plus comfort in times of sorrow, plus the emotional expression that only music can convey, no matter the occasion.

And didn't he look splendid in his U.S. Marine Band uniform, scarlet tunic shimmering with gold braid, contrasting with the light blue trousers tailored to a perfect fit. Almost daily Alta saw him off to play for a White House concert or some big event attended by notables, or perhaps the funeral of an important national leader. Most difficult for Alta were the long, out-of-town engagements. And there were many of them for the band.

His job, glamorous as it was, seldom allowed an evening out with his loving young wife, or a time of fun and games with the children. Fathers weren't playmates in those days. They were – the good ones – role models, disciplinarians, providers. And August was a good one. Alta and the children deeply respected him. They also loved him.

Imagine the family on a typical evening in – to pick a year at random – 1866. The house that August had built ten years earlier was starting to fill up with new Schroeders.

August was 30, Altazera 28. John, the oldest child, was six. (He was my grandfather in years to come.) Frank was four. (He later was engaged to marry my Aunt Gertie – Granny's sister – but he died of

TB before the wedding.) Charlie was about a year old. And Ellie, the first girl, was an infant. Grandmother Dorathea was not yet 50, and still speaking only German. The country was still grieving over the death of Abraham Lincoln and for the hundreds of thousands killed or maimed in the Civil War, that had ended just one year earlier.

After an early dinner, picture them seeing their hero off to his elegant job. Let's say this time the United States Marine Band, under the direction of the noted composer and conductor Francis Maria Scala, was to give a concert in the East Room of the White House. There is evidence that in the Lincoln era the musicians rode to such events in a horse-drawn wagon. After the trolley started running along Pennsylvania Avenue, the men were given tokens to ride it.

The brilliant colors of their uniforms stood out amid the muted tones then popular – dresses of mauve, pale lavender, puce, dark purple. Black gowns trimmed in jet beads were in high style.

The hundreds of flickering candles and a few gas lamps that lit the White House's public rooms cast a magic glow over the guests.

At 524 Ninth Street, just one candle was sputtering in the drafty shaft of the stairwell. Picture Alta carrying that candle in her right hand, with a colicky baby against her left shoulder. It was all the young mother could do to keep her balance up those narrow wedges of stairs, with no way to hold on to the railing. On the small landing at the top, she found Johnny standing there in the dark. He was damp, barefoot, and shivering in the cold air.

"Frank wet the bed," he said in the weary tone of one who had said these words before. They shared the same bed.

Alta laid the baby in her crib and listened helplessly as little Ellie woke, screaming as she drew up her knees in colic pain. The baby would have to wait. Johnny and Frank needed to be taken care of now, wrapped in blankets that would later have to be washed and hung to dry for days, near the wood-burning kitchen stove.

Of course, the boys had to be washed first, with water brought upstairs in a hot kettle. And the bed changed.

Just as Alta was wondering how she would get the time that night to serve August his hot chocolate, after a cold walk from the Pennsylvania Avenue trolley, he came in the door.

"Let me tell you about the concert," he said, giving her a kiss on the cheek. "We were well received – especially for 'Dixie,' which they made us play four times."

Or that's the way it could have been on a night at 524 Ninth in 1866.

August's musical career with the Marine Band prospered through the years, as did Alta's reproductive talents. More and more male children kept coming, and with each one, August's vision for the future grew. He foresaw trios of Schroeders playing chamber music at the city's most elegant gatherings. Then quartets, quintets, sextets, septets and endless varieties of musical groupings, culminating in whole orchestras and big brass bands – all under the Schroeder name.

Each male child was taught to play an instrument or two or three. (Clarence was the exception; he worked for the National Geographic Society).

Girls were arriving, also, in equal numbers with the boys. They were taught to cook.

By 1878, the time was ripe for August to launch his musical empire. After spending 19 great years with the Marine Band, he retired in 1876. He took two years to do the necessary preparations for his second career, and in 1878, he formed the first of the many Schroeder Orchestras and bands that would fill the city and beyond for the next 40 years or more.

It was "The Gilded Age," that elegant era of the late 19th century. The newly rich, dressed in their finest, drove out in carriages behind matched pairs of beautifully groomed horses to mingle with the cream of society. To see and be seen. They built opulent houses that proclaimed their wealth.

As time went on, more and more Schroeder sons took their places in the noted orchestras around town. There were Schroeders in the old Willard Hotel orchestra for 14 years, and even more when the *new* Willard orchestra was formed. August held the baton for both orchestras in their time.

Schroeders also provided music in the parlor of the Ebbitt House and the Raleigh Hotel. They conducted from the pit of the old National Theater plus the Columbia Theater, and the Belasco Theater. Frank, the second son, had great promise, and was in the Academy of Music Orchestra when he died in 1894, at the age of 31.

Schroeder bands and orchestras welcomed outdoor gigs, too – hay rides, sleigh rides, also boat rides down the Potomac on the "W.W. Corcoran" or the "River Queen," where a Schroeder orchestra delighted the passengers with music to dance to or just to accompany the river breezes.

Then, at Marshall Hall, an amusement park down the Potomac past Mount Vernon, another Schroeder orchestra enlivened the scene.

They even played at oyster roasts and corn-husking bees.

If it was splendor you were seeking, however, you went indoors – under the cut crystal chandeliers, shimmering in the candlelight, or gaslight, of the city's ballrooms. Most of them were in the grand hotels downtown, but there were also many in the mansions rising along 16th Street, N.W., near Florida Avenue, long thought of as the city's boundary – socially, at least. Impressive houses of brick and stone were filling large lots along Massachusetts Avenue. Some embassies were beginning to fly their flags on this grand boulevard, each attracting others to join them. Society was moving northwest.

The money to build the private showplaces came from oil, railroads, mega-banks and other treasure troves that were creating new fortunes for entrepreneurs. They gave extravagant parties to show off their wealth. And no party is worth its caviar without music.

Chamber music for a small, elite gathering? We can do that, said the Schroeders.

An orchestra on the ballroom balcony for a debutante's coming-out ball? We can do that, said the Schroeders.

Accompaniment for a dazzling solo violinist? We can do that, said the Schroeders.

And supply the soloist? Of course, said the Schroeders. (The only problem here was whether to send Raymond or Robert as the soloist. Both were Schroeders, naturally.)

The hotels, of course, had a constant need for musicians to supply music for ballroom dancing, background music for dining, and the elegant *thé dansant* for those who had nothing else to do in the late afternoon. The Schroeders were happy – with a lifetime of training – to oblige.

ల

Out of all those years of glamorous engagements, entertaining the rich and famous, only one anecdote trickled down to my generation. It's a rather touching one.

President William McKinley (1897-1901) and his wife Ida frequently came to the Willard Hotel for some relaxation and entertainment. Ida suffered from an illness that rendered her unconscious with no warning.

The first time she had such a "spell" while at the Willard, August Schroeder was conducting the orchestra. He followed his instincts and kept the music flowing, but with misgivings. What should a conductor do when such a notable member of the audience is having a seizure?

He kept his eye on the President, who was covering his wife's face with a large, white handkerchief. Sensing the conductor's dilemma, President McKinley then looked up at August Schroeder, gave him a wave of the hand that said, "Carry on, just as you're doing."

In a few moments, Ida McKinley regained consciousness, and after the President whispered something in her ear, nodded her appreciation to the conductor.

Thereafter, both McKinleys looked toward the orchestra and sent a warm smile in that direction each time they entered the room.

How the blood must have coursed through the veins of those musicians when introducing some brand new masterpiece – "The Beautiful Blue Danube" waltz by the young Johann Strauss, the slightly naughty "Can-Can" from "Orpheus in the Underworld," "The Triumphal March" from Aida, Verdi's instant hit written for the opening of the Suez Canal. Later, the Schroeders – and John Philip Sousa – were also delighted with Scott Joplin's new rage, ragtime music. The old favorite "Dixie" had thrilled crowds both North and South.

At one early 1890s concert in the Midwest, the Sousa band played "Dixie" as an encore after each selection on the program – a total of seven times. The audience went wild with joy.

"Dixie's" popularity paved the way for Sousa's own composition, "Stars and Stripes Forever," the unrivaled top crowd pleaser of today.

And Sousa himself was becoming widely popular for his own new marches that he was playing for audiences all over the world. Sousa, one of the greatest showmen ever born, had a sense of what the people wanted.

Sousa and August Schroeder had a strong bond between them, not just as second-generation neighbors and friends, but also as fellow showmen who enjoyed every note their musicians sounded.

Except for playing music yourself, the only way to hear music in those years was to go where it was being played. And before Sousa there was very little band music.

The less advantaged made their own instruments and played them in whatever time they had left over at the end of the day.

In the Schroeders' world, music set the stage for dancers to glide gracefully over polished ballroom floors to the beat of the latest Viennese waltz. Or race through a sprightly galop or quadrille at breakneck speed.

Long, full skirts of luxurious fabrics rustled to the flowing rhythms, as the escort's white-gloved hand rested ever so lightly at his lady's back.

Most of the men sported luxuriant beards and mustaches, which, or course, must never disturb the even more elaborate hairdos of the "fair sex." The dancing couples kept a discrete distance between the two of them, for decorum as well as for their coiffures.

No matter how handsome the finery and the setting, however, it was the music that breathed life into the scene. Glorious music! The peak years for many of the world's best loved composers: Verdi, Puccini, Brahms, Offenbach, Gilbert (and Sullivan), Tchaikovsky, Liszt, Chopin, Lehar.

August Schroeder's Altazera doubtless heard thousands of bars of music being learned and rehearsed, but I wonder if she ever heard a full orchestra in performance.

Or did she yearn instead – it would be only natural – for the sound of a bathtub filling or a toilet flushing?

CHAPTER 20

THE ZURHORSTS

It all began with Charlemagne.

For the Zurhorsts, at least. They were zur Horsts then, presumably running a dairy farm on the grounds of a monastery at Malgarten, near the city of Osnabrück in the duchy of Hanover (now in Germany).

Charlemagne was crowned the first Holy Roman Emperor on Christmas Day in Rome, in 800 (in an absolutely spectacular coronation). Four years later, in 804 – among a great many other heroic acts – he deeded to the zur Horsts the land they had been occupying, putting into practice his revolutionary view that people have the right to own the land they live on.

That's the story that has been handed down. We haven't heard the Malgarten monks' side.

I didn't know any of this history until my adult years, and tended to think it was a bit grandiose, too dramatic to be true. And then a modern zur Horst appeared. She is Traute zur Horst Stark, who, with her husband, Helmut, was visiting the U.S. As they traveled around this country, she looked for zur Horsts on the last pages of a lot of telephone books. And she found a few Zurhorsts, including a nephew of mine in Columbus, Ohio, Charles Stewart Zurhorst, a son of my late brother.

After a "family reunion" of sorts in Ohio, this distant cousin and her husband came to Washington. During a wonderful day together,

I found that she had happily spent many childhood days with her grandfather zur Horst at the family dairy farm ... in Malgarten.

The family farm – the home of my ancestors for over 1,000 years – still there! In Malgarten. Near Osnabrück in the duchy of Hanover.

We not only had a real life descendent of the original zur Horsts there with us, but she also produced a newspaper clipping of an ad for butter from the zur Horst Dairy Farm in Malgarten. The ad is not dated.

It features the name C. zur Horst (Charles?) next to a non-dairy-looking building that seems to date to the mid-1800s. Below the print is a "Preiscourant" of "I feinste Suprahmbutter." This is followed by what appear to be prices on various quantities of "suprahmbutter" by the pound. All in German, of course.

Nowhere does the ad state that the business was established in 804 A.D.

Life on the farm was not always so bucolic and peaceful as it now appears, however.

Hanover and many of its people paid a terrible price for standing by their convictions during the Reformation. The zur Horsts were Dissenters, firmly in the ranks of those opposed to the excesses of the Roman Church, especially during the 15th, 16th and 17th centuries.

It was a time of enormous upheaval coupled with the unparalleled creativity of the Renaissance.

In 1506 building began on the costly St. Peter's in Rome, with the burden of the expense falling on those least able to afford the price demanded of them. The "them" in 1506 was all of Christendom. There was no possibility of appealing to the state for relief: Church and state were one.

St. Peter's, the biggest church in the world, was built at great cost. Its architects and decorators included Leonardo da Vinci, Raphael, Bernini and Michelangelo. Such talent doesn't come cheap.

The paint was barely dry on Michelangelo's painting of the Sistine Chapel ceiling in St. Peter's when, in 1517, the German monk Martin Luther nailed his 95 theses to a church door in Wittenberg, Germany. This list of the Roman Catholic Church's abuses of its unquestioned authority over the people was the spark that lit the bonfire of the Reformation. Hanover was near the center of the conflagration.

Soon Zwingli took up the cause in Switzerland, followed by Calvin, then Knox in Scotland. Denmark and Norway became committed. Religious wars flared in France, especially against the Protestant Huguenots, thousands of whom were massacred for their faith on St. Bartholomew's Day in 1572.

As rulers across Europe struggled to protect their faith – Catholic or Protestant – a growing number of martyrs were ordered to be burned as heretics.

Meanwhile, Shakespeare was writing *Hamlet*. Rubens, Hals, Van Dyck were at the height of their artistic genius during the Dutch Renaissance, keeping up with Rembrandt who was painting yet another self-portrait, along with his other masterpieces.

In England the Archbishop of Canterbury, Thomas Cranmer, had completed his masterwork, the Anglican *Book of Common Prayer*, before he was burned at the stake. (The nearby charred wooden doorway at Oxford remains as testimony to that deed.)

Mary Tudor ("Bloody Mary") had restored Roman Catholicism to England during her brief and violent reign, 1553-1558. Elizabeth I followed, with a long and also severe rule, 1558-1603, but one filled with daring deeds and high drama. She became the first head of the Church of England, actively involved in steering a course to preserve the core elements of both Catholicism and its Reformation.

After her death in 1603, religion again flared up as an incendiary force in politics. Although the subject had never become dormant, it now became of prime importance in the inter-related politics of England and the continent – eventually reaching into the heart of Hanover itself. The Hanoverian Georges ruled England from 1714 to 1830 simply because they were Protestant descendants of the Roman Catholic Stuarts.

How much did all of this Church and state turmoil affect the everyday lives of the zur Horsts as they milked their cows on the farm in Malgarten, then within the duchy of Hanover?

Did they discuss the Reformation with their old friends, the monks of the Malgarten monastery? Did they dare mention the brutal excesses of the Inquisition?

Where did my ancestors stand with respect to Galileo and his cosmic theories and observations which were condemned by members of the Inquisition? Did they talk about Copernicus and his finding that the earth circled around the sun? The Church called him a heretic for those views. Galileo, too, suffered for using his brain and publicizing his findings.

Did dairy farmers or the average monk discuss such matters? Most people couldn't read in the early days of the Renaissance and the Reformation. It was the printing press that brought enlightenment and power to the common folk, many of whom had their own bibles in their own language, thanks to Zwingli and others like him.

Nor did the early zur Horsts have much of a chance to see a Rembrandt painting or a Michelangelo sculpture. There was precious little leisure time for the average man or woman.

But there was no way to escape the religious upheaval and human suffering of the 16th and 17th centuries. By 1618 the violence of faith had turned into full-fledged war. It raged within Germany for the most part. And it lasted for 30 years.

The zur Horsts had stood their ground as Dissenters for as long as they could, but at the start of the Thirty Years War in 1618, my ancestors left a devastated Hanover and moved to Holland, where they stayed for the length of that conflict.

Within those 30 years, what is now Germany was invaded by French, Swedish and Danish forces. In that space of time, over half the people of Hanover and the surrounding lands were massacred or succumbed to a plague that swept the region.

The zur Horsts I can claim as direct forefathers returned to Holland after a few miserable years in the decimated homeland, and then, in the late 1600s, made a major and permanent break from Hanover. They moved to Waterford, Ireland.

The Old Order was changing drastically in the 16th and 17th centuries. Not only was the faith of the fathers in upheaval, but also the fatherland – the ancestral home from as far back as memory reaches – was losing its hold on sons and daughters, as many took off for new worlds and lands unknown. It was as if the old world seemed too broken to be fixed, and the only hope was to get a new start in the New World.

The Irish zur Horsts – now known as Zurhorsts – didn't go directly to the American colonies as so many of the English did; they went by stages.

Charles Frederick Zurhorst, my great-grandfather,
with unidentified child (standing) and toddler
George Pickford Zurhorst, my grandfather, circa 1862.

And even though they apparently remained in Waterford for at least two generations, they left few clues behind. Or maybe I didn't know where to look.

But I'll never forget the clerk's face when I asked for any information available in the Irish records on my ancestor Hermann Zurhorst. As I stood among Kellys and O'Briens and Fitzgeralds in a Waterford office, I could feel suspicious eyes on me. *Hermann Zurhorst, indeed; you'd be expectin' to find the likes of him here?*

The closest I came to tracking him down was among the records of a small Protestant church in Waterford. On a faded list of Dissenters who had contributed to the church in the early 1700s, there he was: Hermann Zurhorst.

Someone had handwritten on the paper: "Note the number of English surnames, with the exotic exception of Hermann Zurhorst."

Eventually – after two or three generations in Ireland – some Zurhorsts moved to London, England, and then to Guernsey, in the Channel Islands, where several are buried.

Charles Frederick Zurhorst finally made the giant leap of faith to the United States of America. His first home in this country was in Morristown, N.J., where he and Mary Ann Easton were married in St. Peter's Episcopal Church. For unknown reasons they resettled in Martinsville, Indiana, before Charles Frederick joined the Union Army in 1862. He served in the war as a cabinetmaker and undertaker, based in Washington, D.C., near the Capitol.

In 1866, he was to purchase a building that *The Washington Post* has called "one of the most important, valuable sites left on the Hill" – 301 East Capitol.

CHAPTER 21

THE OTHER ZURHORSTS

In December 2006, my adult daughter Susanna and I were searching desperately for a parking place somewhere near a restaurant – any restaurant – on Pennsylvania Avenue, S.E.

After 20 minutes or more, a car pulled out of a tight space just off the avenue, and we squeezed into the opening.

It wasn't until we had eaten half of our lunch that I looked through the window next to our table. And there it was – my *bete noire* of a building – 203 Third Street, looming as menacing as ever.

I had to remind myself that the malignant spell it had cast over me was now benign, rescinded and redeemed by later generations as innocent of the family dynamics as I had been.

"Look behind you," I said to Susanna. "That's your great-grandfather Zurhorst's house." She turned to look.

"What was he like? I never knew anything about him."

"I didn't know much. He died before I was born." This wasn't the time or the place to go into the details.

I glanced away. And then found myself facing, through an opposite window overlooking Pennsylvania Avenue, the building where my father, Charles Stewart Zurhorst, had been born. I wondered if Papa had ever been inside the home built by his father, George P.: The house at 203 Third, just two blocks from where we had lived, at 301 East Capitol. Southeast, of course.

We were at Ground Zero of the Zurhorst family history. Here's where the trouble began.

Finding a parking space in that part of Capitol Hill on a pre-Christmas Saturday was remarkable. But finding that particular space at the heart of a journey into our past seemed predestined, beyond coincidence.

And who would have thought that this family mystery swirling like an autumn fog around 203 Third would eventually find a solution as far away as Key West, Florida? Over three generations later.

Susanna and I didn't just happen to be lunching or shopping on Capitol Hill that day. Suddenly aware that she has forebears, she had come all the way from her home in northern California to visit both me and her ancestors. Or rather to see where they had lived – mostly within a ten-block area on Capitol Hill (Southeast only). Since 1840.

We had been by the 150-year-old Schroeder homestead at 524 Ninth Street, built shortly after the death of her maternal great-great-great grandfather, Christian Schroeder, just up the street from the U.S. Marine Barracks.

Of course, we had to drive by John Philip Sousa's birthplace, a few paces away from the Marine Barracks on G Street. The Sousas and Schroeders had been neighbors and friends for many years. The nearby Christ Episcopal Church was the historic mother church to many parishes in the diocese.

And, although there is no plaque to proclaim the event, this is the church that Granny left to join the vast ranks of the unchurched, and never looked back.

The mysterious house at 203 Third Street, S.E. (present day).

George Pickford Zurhorst, my grandfather.

In the early 1900s, Granny and Grandpap and their only child, my mother, Edwinetta, attended Christ Church. At that time, they lived across Ninth Street from the ancestral Schroeder home.

One day as the ladies of the parish were making sandwiches for some Marines who were coming to a "tea party," Granny was scolded by one of the ladies for buttering both pieces of bread, instead of one. "That's wasteful," said the guild member, according to family lore.

"And buttering only one slice is cheap," Granny answered, putting down the butter knife and walking out of the parish hall forevermore.

"I refuse to belong to a cheap church," she often explained, with a touch of self-righteousness.

There was probably no connection between that incident and the family's move to Seward Square, a few blocks away, bordering Pennsylvania Avenue, but move they did.

Susanna and I had a hard time finding the exact house because of the layout of that part of the avenue.

We had no difficulty, of course, locating the next home of Granny and Grandpap, at 318 A Street, where I was born and visited so frequently.

We drove by St. Mark's and St. Cecilia's, and Mr. Johnnie's, and Grubb's Pharmacy and Union Station, and homes of long-gone relatives who left only sketchy memories behind.

And, of course, in our roamings, we passed 301 East Capitol – now a Folger annex – many times, and yearned to go in, but there was no place to park.

Never, though, was 203 Third Street on the itinerary. Subconsciously, I supposed, I was still avoiding this "Dracula's Castle" of my childhood. Yet it – or something – drew me to it, with the opening up of the only parking space for blocks around. That's the way I felt when I realized where we were.

A complex set of circumstances formed and then perpetuated the mystery of 203 Third. They add up to an explanation only after years of retrospection. Clues here and there for over three generations didn't make sense until the end, as it were.

I can remember, very vaguely, being told not to ask Grandma Zurhorst questions about her life before she came to live at Granny's on A Street.

No one explained why not. Although I doubt that I ever asked. (I was the kind of child who didn't ask such questions; I preferred to try and figure out the answers for myself.)

Who would have connected this gentle, soft-spoken little Scotswoman with the aura of evil that I imagined emanating from 203 Third? Had she lived there?

There were other clues that I missed until I could look back on them as they came together gradually. Clues such as hearing Aunt Gertie telling Granny that she had seen "the second Mrs. Zurhorst down on the avenue." She sniffed as she said it.

Typically, I didn't inquire further, but I thought a lot about this odd statement. (Children should be seen and not heard was the prevailing law.) How could there be a "second Mrs. Zurhorst?"

Did I have two mothers? How many Mrs. Zurhorsts could there be? By this time, somehow, I had learned that 203 was a Zurhorst place. Was this where a lot of Mrs. Zurhorsts lived? Like a harem? What awful things went on in that tall, scary heap of masonry?

Was the little boy with the Argyle socks one of *them*? I don't recall when or where we met; I just remember his beautiful socks and heavy woolen suit with the self-belted jacket and knickerbocker pants, gathered at the knee. He was about eight years old, and good looking. Mama introduced him to Brother and me as "your cousin, Walls."

Later, I asked Brother who he was, and Brother didn't know either.

Granny commented that he was "a surprisingly well-behaved child," as if she had expected a monster. "Very polite, nice little boy," Mama rather reluctantly agreed.

Although Walls had lived just two blocks south of where we lived – both of us over Zurhorst funeral parlors – I didn't see him again for over 40 years.

Within that time, I had graduated from the University of Maryland, moved to Silver Spring, Maryland, married, had two children, and 14 years later, in 1963, was divorced.

In the early '70s, my former husband Bob phoned me with the news that he had found "some Zurhorsts" in Key West, Florida, while he was on vacation. He met them at a cocktail party.

I had no idea who they could be, but I called someone named Betty Bruce in Key West. She had given Bob her number and wanted me to phone her.

Just minutes into the conversation, I felt an easy rapport with this stranger. She explained that she was Rosina's daughter.

But who was Rosina?

The only time I had heard the name Rosina was as a high-spirited character in Rossini's "The Barber of Seville."

Then Betty said she had a surprise for me. Another voice came on the line – a strangely youthful voice, cheerful and light-hearted. "This is your Aunt Rosina. Your father's sister. I loved Charley dearly."

Papa's *sister*?

I had been barely six years old when Papa had died. How could I be talking to his sister? The only sister of his that I knew of was Aunt Mary, and she, too, had been dead for many years. The "other Zurhorsts" had long since disappeared from Capitol Hill.

Both Betty and then Aunt Rosina begged me to come to Key West. But first they wanted me to meet some young cousins who lived less than a mile from my home in the Maryland suburbs.

Wary and confused, I telephoned my brother in Maine to see if he had any more information about these lost relatives than I did. He didn't but added, casually, that we had lost touch with "that side of the family after the divorce."

"What divorce?" I asked.

"Papa's parents," he said. "Don't you remember? You knew about that, didn't you? We weren't supposed to mention it, but we knew about it. ... Or maybe *you* didn't. Mama and Granny told me a few years after Papa died. They said they would tell you when you were old enough to understand."

I drew a deep breath. "Well, they never did."

"It happened a long time ago," he said. "Before either of us was born." He, in a sense, was dismissing the reality that confronted me in the flesh.

"How would you feel if you were to come face-to-face with a close relative you had never known existed?"

"Don't make a production of it," he urged in his Big Brother tone of voice. "It belongs to the past. Forget it."

I had no intention of forgetting any part or any one from this unexpected turn in my life.

⁓

Next stop was the young cousins who lived so close to me and my family now. When I telephoned them, they indicated – without a great deal of conviction – that they would be happy to see me. But, frankly, they sounded as confused as I was.

I could almost hear them talk as I drove to their house: "*Mary* Zurhorst? Who is *she*? Aunt Rosina (or Tobey or Betty or Grandmother or Mother and Daddy) never spoke of a Mary Zurhorst."

The two young women and their brother were gracious, but they were staring at me as if I had just stepped out of a UFO. I'm sure I was looking just as perplexed at them.

Trying to figure where this group fit into our small family, I asked if they were Aunt Rosina's grandchildren.

"Oh, no. She's our great-aunt. *Our* grandmother was Mamie," they said in a ragged chorus.

"Mamie Walls!" I exclaimed, finally recognizing a name from the past.

"Oh, then you must have known her."

"No, not at all," I said.

Confusion squared.

I asked who their mother and father were.

"Jane and Buzz," they answered.

We were getting nowhere. I'd never heard of Jane and Buzz. I began to be aware of the fact that nobody had asked me a single question. It was like being a ghost.

Unasked, I started to introduce them to my side of the family. "My father was Charles Stewart Zurhorst. He and his sister Mary were the children of George P. and Emma McGowan Zurhorst."

A few jaws dropped but there was utter silence.

I went on. "George and Emma were divorced." Instant eye contact shot around the room. There were outcries of "Wait a minute," "Hold it."

I plodded ahead, just because I had the momentum and I couldn't stop.

"He remarried. I knew his second wife only as the 'second Mrs. Zurhorst.' I never knew her given name. In fact, I never saw her. But you all must have come from this second marriage." Outcries of "NO! NO!" Then, "There's never been a divorce in our family. I know that for certain."

In a moment of befuddled silence, I asked who they thought I was.

One answered, perplexed, "We don't know *who* you are." All eyes were peering at me, guileless, clueless.

"Did anyone in your family ever mention Charles, my father?"

They exchanged glances. One volunteered that Aunt Rosina had spoken of a Charley with affection. He was an uncle or maybe a distant cousin, they thought. Word was that there had been a Charley in the family, but he died and never married or had children. "He was a playboy."

Another volunteered that George P. had had several children, all of whom had died young except for Rosina and a son George, who married Mamie Walls. They had a son, nicknamed Buzz, who was father to this young group.

"From what we heard," the brother said, "Great-grandmother Zurhorst wouldn't have tolerated a divorce in the family. And Grandmother Mamie considered divorce a mortal sin."

"These were very moral women," another voice spoke up.

One of the sisters said earnestly, "That's why I feel so bad now. I'm in the middle of getting a divorce, and it's bringing disgrace down on the family. The first Zurhorst ever to be divorced." There were tears of shame in her eyes.

I gently repeated the family history, including the divorce, but nothing I said seemed to register.

Before I left, mission unaccomplished, one of these young cousins shared a different version of my father's disappearance from the family. In this story, Charles had been offered the family business, but, being a playboy, he wasn't interested. So young George got the business – at 203 Third Street – and Charley got a yacht. He sailed away on it and was never heard of again. So who occupied 301 East Capitol – with "Zurhorst" in gold lettering on the window? It was my father, of course, Charles Stewart Zurhorst.

I was beginning to dread the promised trip to meet the Key West branch of the family. What had they been told? And by whom? Was the cover-up of the divorce all-pervasive?

I needn't have worried. When I met Aunt Rosina, then in her 80s, she was as trim and attractive – and loving – as she must have been in her early 20s when she visited Key West and found a dashing young Benjamin Curry Moreno there. He was descended from the original Spanish settlers in Key West. She married him five weeks later (in 1917) and never regretted it. And never left. She lived to be 93.

She spoke endearingly of her half-brother, my father, and delighted in knowing me. She seemed untouched by the stories passed on by others to the next generation, stories that dismissed my father.

Our moving reunion was enhanced by the rapport between Aunt Rosina's daughter, Betty Bruce, and me. First cousins? Once-removed? Step-cousins? Half-cousins? We weren't sure, and it didn't matter. We were soul mates.

Betty's impishly funny husband, Toby Bruce, was a buddy of Ernest Hemingway, who hung out with the Bruces whenever he was in Key West. Many Hemingway papers were entrusted to the Bruces and thus preserved.

The first night I was there, Betty called together the Key West Zurhorsts for a family gathering. (We couldn't call it a reunion; we hadn't been together before.) How could these wonderful people have originated from my old nemesis of brick and stone, 203 Third Street?

One member of the third generation of Zurhorsts in Key West told me that she had always thought of 203 Third Street as being spooky, even though she had never seen it. She said she had asked Buzz, who had lived there, if he had been scared, living over the funeral parlors. But he said "no." Then she told me that she had heard that George P. had had tunnels and cave-like spaces dug under Pennsylvania Avenue to store the remains in before burial. It was always cold down there.

I didn't follow up on the story. And neither did she.

I was having difficulty sorting out these Zurhorsts when a dynamic, handsome man in his early 50s or so took my hand and led me across the courtyard of the Bruce home to Aunt Rosina's exquisite, classic old Key West mansion next door.

"We have some family treasures to share," he smiled.

We crossed broad, lush verandas, rooms cool and dark, with thick rugs and fireplaces. Over one fireplace, an heirloom portrait of a dramatic, Regency creature, bedecked in scarves and fancy trimmings, done by a first-class artist. She had a flirtatious half-smile on her face – a sort of preview of Aunt Rosina.

"May I present our great-great-grandmother, Ann Judith Williams Zurhorst, of the Isle of Guernsey, Channel Islands."

The Channel Islands. How romantic.

Then this man – Buzz, he was called – suggested we sit down in front of the portrait and go over a leather-bound notebook he was holding, wrapped carefully in a linen cloth. The dry and crumbly pages were just barely legible.

"This is the travel journal of our great-grandfather, Charles Frederick Zurhorst, Ann Judith's son," he told me. "After she died, Charles Frederick, then a U.S. citizen, sailed back to England in 1862 to 'save' the portrait." Was there some dire threat to snatch it away from the family? Who was the woman with the French name fleetingly mentioned among family matters in this journal? Did she figure in the swift action to save the portrait?

Buzz read aloud some of Charles Frederick's notes to himself for the trip ("get parrot," "presents for Octavia," "see friends in Fleet Street"), some corny jokes, and then news of his time in London before going to Guernsey to get his mother's picture. The drama increased with violent force on the return trip when the weather turned wicked, sweeping men overboard, breaking masts, and driving icebergs into the ship.

Throughout the journal, Charles Frederick kept his calm, and even his sense of humor. I was tremendously moved to hear of this trip from one of his great-grandsons. It was as if my – our – great-grandfather himself were reading it aloud.

That moment will stay with me forever. But I still wasn't sure who this charming Buzz was, with the same forebears as I had.

"What was your name before it was Buzz?" I finally asked.

He laughed. "Bern*ard* Walls Zurhorst."

Bernard Walls, the "well-behaved little boy" in the knicker-bocker pants and Argyle socks. The cousin from 203 Third, whom even Granny begrudgingly admired.

One of *them*. My God.

The son of Mamie Walls Zurhorst, to whom Granny had barely given a nod in greeting in Woodward & Lothrop's elevator.

Grandson of our grandfather, George Pickford Zurhorst. Father of the three young cousins I had confused in Silver Spring, Maryland, who weren't sure I really existed.

Son of the "moral" Mamie. Grandson of "the second Mrs. Zurhorst," who, together with Mamie, her daughter-in-law, had woven the myth of my father's disappearance to cover up the fact of the divorce.

A giant cover-up pulled off successfully among many offspring – but not all – for over 70 years.

And here was, despite it all, such a fine, admirable man, my cousin, who was bringing me into the other half of the family with open arms. And open mind.

And *my* mind was being pried wide open, too.

How could he and his lovely wife Jane belong to *that* side of the family? Or Aunt Rosina and Betty? Were they *them*?

Well, thank God that before their time was up, we became us. One family. Including my father Charley and my brother Charley, even in absentia. Might as well count "the second Mrs. Zurhorst" and Mamie Walls as family, too. They probably had their own reasons for redefining the Zurhorst family.

Linda Carter, Betty's daughter (great-granddaughter of "the second Mrs. Zurhorst," granddaughter of Rosina) now does more than keep in touch, especially in working on this book. We're on the phone often – Silver Spring to Key West – exchanging ancient and current family news. My young cousin whom I met in Silver Spring, now remarried, has shed her imposed guilt about divorce in the family, now that the truth has made her free.

There is also tangible proof of reunion and reconciliation among the Zurhorsts. Linda called one night to say that there was a package in the mail for me. From all of them.

In the mailing were two worn leather booklets: One was the cherished travel journal written by Charles Frederick Zurhorst in 1862, and read aloud to me by Buzz.

The other was a tiny, charmingly innocent diary kept by Aunt Rosina when she was 18, in 1913. Selections are included in this book.

Who could have predicted that I would be the one to get them? After generations of separation, now affection and harmony. Two policies: "Don't ask; don't tell" and "Deny and destroy the evidence." Neither worked.

Unanswered questions: Whose spirit led Susanna and me to the parking space in front of 203 Third? Was it Grandfather George P. in a penitential mood? Or the "second Mrs. Zurhorst" and Mamie up to a bit of mischief?

And who led my ex-husband to that Key West cocktail party? We'll never know, will we?

CHAPTER 22

EXCERPTS FROM C.F. ZURHORST'S JOURNAL

When Buzz and I were reading our great-grandfather's travel journal together in the mid-1970s, most of it was still legible, although many passages were faded beyond recognition. Now, over 30 years later, all but an occasional word appears in pale, ghostly form, unreadable.

Thanks to the reprinting of much of it in *The New York Times* Travel Section on Sunday, May 13, 1979, however, it is preserved in the archives of that newspaper. I think Charles Frederick would have been pleased.

Excerpted in *The Times*, the journal begins: "Took passage Oct. 25th, '61. Passenger (fare $30) for Liverpool, England, on board Steam Ship Aetna, 2,200 tons. Capt. [illegible] late of Great Eastern. Obtained passport of Oscar Irving, 36½ Pine Street, N.Y."

Within 12 uneventful days, they steamed into Liverpool. His passport application describes him as 39 years old, 5 feet 11½ inches; blue eyes, dark hair. He was born in London on July 8, 1822. On his birthday in 1858, he became a citizen of the United States in Morgan County, Indiana.

In place of the signature of a witness, his passport application says, "See letter from G.P. Morton, Gov. of Indiana, to the Hon. Chas. F. Adams, Minister to England."

Charles Frederick Zurhorst had grown up in London, and, after his father's recent death, he was returning to England to settle the estate and to bring back to the U.S. his mother's portrait. It was on the Isle of Guernsey where the family had been living after they had left London.

According to his notes, Charles Frederick touched base with a number of friends in London before going on to Guernsey. He was entertained up and down Fleet Street by old friends there (Had he been a journalist?), went to the theater with them, to museums and galleries and to many homes, where, apparently, he was warmly welcomed.

His business taken care of quickly on Guernsey – he didn't seem to want to linger – he set sail on February 19, 1862, "bound for New York via Liverpool, per Steam Ship City of New York, over 2,560 tons."

Here is the hair-raising account of that journey in his own words.

Five days out, headwinds all the way, with a heavy surf blowing great guns ... women and children sad and lonesome.

First day after starting, one sailor swept off quarterdeck with leg broken. Left him at Queenstown next day. Steward thrown down, broken rib and dislocated arm.

Crowded with passengers, men, women and children of all nationalities. On Friday evening, gratitude and Psalm singing.

Monday 25th. Wind strong N.W. carried away main topsail with tremendous crash. Very little sickness. Not at all sick myself. Very *home*sick. Almost crazy to see wife and little ones. Every hour a day, every day a week.

Rock, rock. Shipping sea after sea. Not a dry plank since we left Liverpool. To bed at 9 o'clock. Lay all night in water. Drip, drip, drip. Changed sides to get dry. Quilts soaking.

26th. Woke up wet, sore throat and sick headache – not with seasickness, but with violent cold. Heavy sea rolling.

Wednesday, 27th. Moderating, not so rough. Lay to 14 hours to fix machinery. Dead loss of time. Very lonesome these nights. Hear plenty of sighing from male and female.

Thursday, 28th. Wind ahead. Sea rough – nothing new. Had conversation with gent in steerage who has just returned with wife and five children from a second voyage to and from Australia! He represents Australia as the friendliest country. He had a very bad cold and was seasick.

Friday, 29th. Weather pleasant. Made a fine run, set all sails at sunset and ran like a bird until 8 o'clock when we struck an iceberg. Great consternation on board. Screaming among females and moaning on deck by the men. Took in all sails, stopped engines, cleared the bergs. Went slow speed and kept in field of ice and danger all night.

Considerable excitement caused by man coming down in cabin with news that we were going down and the vessel parting. But all humbug. The man was frightened and supposed Gabriel had blown the horn.

Went to sleep and left to that Providence (who has always guarded me) the matter to bestow, if He thought proper.

To tell the truth, fears at this time never entered my breast, but a desire for safety was my prayer and in case of death my dear wife and little ones might be protected.

Saturday. Woke at 6 o'clock, washed and dressed. Very cold on the banks of Newfoundland.

Sea smooth ... Bergs of every size continue on both bows; of beautiful patterns and magnificent structure. At last, quite clear, and weather moderating.

Sunday. Weather like a May morning. At 10 o'clock bell ringing – church to be held for all willingly to attend (in the main cabin). Public worship of the Church of England, led in a beautiful style by the Captain.

It is indeed a solemn matter to attend Divine Worship at sea. The sailors all shaved and clean dressed and the passengers of all nationalities paying tribute and glorifying One God! ...

Tuesday ... Ate good breakfast and thought of dear ones at home, and the prospect of once more embracing the idol of my heart.

Afternoon. Eyes bad, almost blind. Heavy sea, strong gale headwind.

[The writing becomes almost illegible; there is no entry for Wednesday.]

Thursday O.K. by noon ... At night, all on deck watching for Sandy Hook Light. Happy thoughts of home strong, and suspense great. Fine night. Everybody in good humor, glad at prospect of landing.

Here some lines are not readable. They are followed by "offered sincere and very [illegible] upon Bar Keeper."

Land in view! Sandy Hook. Made Fort Lafayette. The look on proud pilot's face glorious.

News of success of the Federals hailed from end to end of the ship. Hurrah, hurrah for the Union . . .

Abundance of ice on North River. Arrived safe at Castle Gardens March 6, after 15 days of voyage.

March 7th left N.Y. by Erie R.R., for the Land of the West and the home of my choice, by 5 o'clock express train.

Saturday morning train shoved off track ... Snowing fast. Detained at Dunkirk from 3 P.M. until 1½ A.M. by losing connection in aforesaid accident. Arrived at Cleveland, Ohio, Sunday A.M. at 7 o'clock. No train until Monday morning (two dear days lost in consequence of one hour's delay as Sunday travel is stopped). Went to church at Methodist Episcopal. Heard a good sermon. Cleveland, a populous city, very quiet on Sunday. Well built and of a thriving character. Scarcely a store of any description with shutters up, speaking well for the quiet and honesty of the inhabitants.

Very homesick. Almost crazy to see wife and little ones... Stopping at City Hotel, H. H. & H. Co. Brick wing projection. Monday 10th. Woke up in good spirits but with bad cold. News boy at foot of hotel stairs with morning papers (great institution). Glorious Victory of our troops at Leesburg. Hurrah for the Union and the Stars and Stripes. Leave here for Indianapolis at 8 A.M. almost in a state of suspense to see *Home, Sweet Home*.

Changed cars three times from N.Y. to Indpls.: Dunkirk, Cleveland & Crestline. Crossed the Ohio Line into Indiana at 5 P.M. Hurrah for the Hoosier State. Arrived safe at Indianapolis at 9 o'clock P.M. and hailed the city with delight.

It was March 1862; he was to join the Union troops at Antietam a few months after returning home. Although he survived the war, he died, as far as we know, in Washington, D.C., in about 1873.

CHAPTER 23

ROSINA'S DANDY LIFE

The entry for 30 January, Thursday, 1913, in Alice Rosina Zurhorst's diary reads: "Birthday – 18 Years old ...

"Stayed home from school. Miss Lehman here making me a velvet suit. I embroidered nearly all day. In afternoon Ma, Freda and I went down town [sic]. Freda took me to the Col. to see Julia Sanderson in 'The Sunshine Girl.' The show was fine and she is a dear.

"Mr. Parker and Mr. Sweeney each gave me a dandy box of candy.

"In eve. Wrote three letters."

Rosina was the petite and bubbly daughter of George Pickford Zurhorst (my grandfather) and his second wife, Elizabeth Stunden. They lived at 203 Third Street, S.E., over the funeral home run by George P., which was only two blocks from the funeral home run by my father, Charles S., at 301 East Capitol.

Charley and Rosina refused to take part in the not-so-genteel feud between the Zurhorst businesses, and between the Zurhorsts who came *before* the divorce, and those who came after the divorce. They were deeply fond of each other.

Since I wasn't born until 1919, I missed out on the height of the rivalry. By then, Rosina had literally sailed off into the sunset, never to return from Key West, and George P. had died.

The sibling fondness that Charley felt for his little half-sister was shared romantically by many chaps who flocked to her house day and night (rarely past 10:30 p.m.), bearing "dandy" boxes of candy, and bouquets of sweet peas and bunches of violets, as reported in her diary.

Rosina was always on the go, with plenty of male and female friends to go with. Occasionally, she casually mentions going to school between trips to down town, and to the nearby "5¢ show," almost daily dramas at downtown theaters, jaunts with "Ma" and Freda to the Ave. Grand (Pennsylvania Avenue, S.E.) and endless walks through Capitol Hill. But rarely to school. She did, though, put a lot of time into learning embroidery. And writing in her diary.

After she "cleaned up," (the house, presumably) she notes on Jan, 4 that "Geo and Jack in for a few min. About 1 p.m. Freda and I went down town. When I got home Ethelyn was here. Later I dressed and Samuel and John Whiley (?) came about 6:30. Freda came and we had dinner. Left about 8 p.m. for the theatre. 'The Merry Widow' at the Belasco. Very Good.

"After show went for a nice ride in the machine. Just as we [got to] the house, had a blow out. S and F came in and we had cider and cake."

Some squiggles – like hieroglyphics – at the bottom of the page, and followed in very small letters by the word "Joke." And beneath that, almost falling off the page: "Letter from Fox."

The next day, she went to Sunday school, and wrote to Fox. Also wrote to Skeet. That afternoon, Mrs. O'Brien came by, and Freda was in for a while. Then, "Ma" walked Mrs. O'Brien home. "Helen Springman came in. Mr. Lou and Dave Diggins here for few minutes.

Aunt Rosina, at about age 18.

"About 8:30 W. Schwartz, Johnnie Ligon & Geo. Garland came. Lots of music and fun all eve. Boys left about 11:30. Helen stayed in all night."

On January 9, Sam K. took her to the National Theatre to see Rose Stahl play "Maggie Pepper." Rosina declares it "Great." After the show, they went for a ride. "Had a dandy time."

The next day, after school, Rosina and Freda had "lots of fun" down town. "In eve. Johnnie Liggon, Helen Springman, Willie S. & I went to Co. D dance at Dyer's. Had lots of fun …."

On January 11, a Saturday, Rosina chronicles a sorority meeting in the afternoon – "Lots of fun" – followed by a visit from Sam K. They played rhum (sic) until about 9:30 p.m., when Sam and Rosina and Freda (the ubiquitous Freda) decided to go for a ride "out Bladensburg road, and didn't have Md. License. Just across the line saw a big fat man who we thought was the sheriff. Thought we would find a road to go around & lead into the city without passing him. Got lost, roads terribly muddy. Went just about 6 mi. from Annapolis …. Had packs of fun."

The next day (January 12) Rosina and her usual brood of friends piled in a car and drove to Arlington, where they had a puncture "but fun."

Rosina *always* had fun, whether it was pulling taffy, dancing, going to Sunday school, riding around in the "machine" or the horsedrawn Victoria, going downtown to shop, making "coco," theatre-going almost nightly, and almost always with Freda Van Nest.

After the show, Mr. Sweeny generally shows up, and occasionally drives them home, in his blowout-prone machine. (When Rosina uses the word "car," she is referring to streetcar). No, he was not a chauffeur, this Mr. Sweeny. Read on in the diary and learn that Rosina frequently received boxes of candy ("dandy") and bunches of violets or pink sweet peas from Mr. Sweeny. And more of the same from numerous other young men who swarmed around her, like bees to the honeyed hive.

One night (February 6, to be precise), after Rosina had her picture taken at Harris and Ewings (sic), followed by "something to eat at Reeves, Mr. Sweeny brought us some fried oysters. Made Ma and I both sick."

This item not followed by the usual "Lots of fun."

Various entries give us peeks into pre-World War I social life, which Rosina lived to the fullest. All of it "lots of fun," according to her tiny, very feminine handwriting.

"Called up the stable for a carriage," she notes. Mrs. O'Brien, Mamie, Ma and Rosina "went for a drive."

Freda and she saw "Chauncey Alcott in 'The isle of Dreams'," along with the ubiquitous Mr. Sweeny, who sent Freda violets and Rosina pink sweet peas. A few days later, Mr. Barker and Mr. Sweeny each gave her a "dandy box of candy." The following day, Hubert Shinn sent her an equally "dandy box of candy."

On February 2, 1913, after noting that the groundhog had seen his shadow, Rosina tells that Freda's father "sent us a swell Victoria and we went out to Alvin's Drug Store, then out to call on Irma Reichard, then through Rock Creek Park and the Zoo, out around Lincoln Park and home."

On March 3 – a "beautiful day" – Rosina went to the Suffragette parade. The next day, she went up the street to the Capitol to see Woodrow Wilson inaugurated.

She seemed far more delighted when she and her friends – eight of them – spent an evening shelling nuts, and the next night salting them.

They all seemed to be in constant motion, these male and female friends of Rosina's, alighting here and there, dropping by for a quick visit, and then, like a gaggle of geese, all following when one changed direction. Sometimes, after a sociable evening of dancing or singing at Rosina's house, the visitors walked each other home, all over Capitol Hill. "Lots of fun."

She writes on July 31, 1913. "Wrote letters ... Had the blues all eve, and mosquitoes so bad that I didn't sleep but very little."

Just three years later, Rosina met the romantic love of her life in Key West, where they lived happily for the rest of her many years. "Lots of fun."

CHAPTER 24

THE RISE AND FALL OF A CAREER

The 1904 D.C. City Directory lists my father's sister Mary as a "typewriter." There is no hint of how meteoric her business career would be, especially its explosive ending.

Following their parents' divorce, Mary Arline and her younger brother Charles, both in their early 20's, were living with their mother at 409 C Street, S.E., Seward Square.

Just a block or so up Pennsylvania Avenue, S.E., stood 203 Third Street, the imposing home of their father, George P. Zurhorst and his second wife, the former Elizabeth Stunden.

One year later, in 1905, Mary started the National Cooking School at the Seward Square house, Mary A. Zurhorst, Principal. By the next year, Mary moved the school and her mother and brother to the posh lower Connecticut Avenue area, sensing and leading the trend for the city's development toward northwest, rather than eastward from Capitol Hill, as was originally planned by developers.

The school and family of three soon relocated to 1718 Q Street, N.W. (Fifty-seven years later, when my former husband and I went our separate ways, he moved into 1718 Q Street, unaware of the connection.)

From 1905 through 1920, Aunt Mary's school moved at least five times within the popular new neighborhood.

By 1915, just eleven years after she had started a "cooking school" in her Seward Square home, this self-trained young woman landed in the Big Leagues: She acquired Mount Alto.

This property was among the most desirable in the city.

Situated on a hill overlooking Washington and Georgetown, Mount Alto was the setting for "one of the most elegant dwellings to be found in our borders," according to the *Georgetown Courier*. The site faces Wisconsin Avenue, above Reservoir Road.

According to ads in the *Washington Star* in 1916, the 12-acre campus of The National School of Domestic Arts and Science at Mount Alto was to contain a total of 11 buildings by 1918, including community units where students could be trained in domestic arts and science, greenhouses and conservatories, six tennis courts and other spaces designed for exercise and recreation facilities, plus dormitories. The school was being planned to serve 200 boarding and 400 day students.

The total financial investment was estimated to be $1,000,000.

The architect and co-owner of the school was Charles Francis Wood, who had built cadet barracks at West Point and officers' quarters at the Annapolis Naval Academy.

Suddenly, the grandiose plans for the school halted. Instead of dorms and tennis courts, the Federal Government erected a veterans hospital on the property, to house injured soldiers from World War I.

(In 1969, the Soviet Union purchased Mount Alto. It is now the Russian Embassy.)

In 1915, Aunt Mary moved her school into seven houses she had remodeled near Connecticut and Rhode Island Avenue, N.W. After a few more short-term relocations, she packed it all in and took off for New Rochelle, New York, where she and her business partner Charles Wood developed a community of elegant homes for the wealthy.

Papa's sister, Mary Arline, who sent us the alligator and the lamb.

The posh development inspired the song, "Forty-five Minutes From Broadway," which is how long it took the commuter train to get there from Grand Central.

The development was called Wykagyl Park.

Some time in this buying frenzy, she bought a house in Tampa, Florida. In a rare showing of familial affection, she sent us a souvenir from there – a tiny, live alligator, which we named "Blinky." We kept it until it grew to almost two feet long. We then donated it to the Washington Zoo.

Papa warned her never to send another present like Blinky to a family that lived in a third-floor apartment over the funeral parlors. At least Blinky was quiet.

She responded some time later by sending us a baby lamb, so young it had to be fed from a baby's bottle. Fortunately, he arrived just as we were leaving to spend our first summer at the Leonardtown house. So York accompanied us on the steamboat. He grew to be a huge, curly-horned ram. When he butted Grandpap into the side of the barn one day, he was sent to live at a farm down toward Tall Timbers.

In 1926, Aunt Mary became ill and spent her last days with her sister-in-law, my mother, at 301 East Capitol, over the parlors.

She had become a very wealthy woman. She often told Mama that she had left everything to her and my brother and me.

Although she had died in December of 1926, by summer of 1927, we still had heard nothing from those managing her estate, despite inquiries.

Finally, while we were at the house in Leonardtown that summer, Aunt Mary's business partner, Charles Wood, telephoned to say he was in Washington and was going to rent a car so that he could come and see us about the inheritance.

As he walked in the door, a mirror that had belonged to Aunt Mary slid silently down the wall. The hook remained intact, the glass unshattered.

Mr. Wood told us that he had to clear up a few details, but that the check would be in the mail within the next few days. He returned to New Rochelle.

Two days later, a member of his family called from New Rochelle to tell us that Charles Wood had committed suicide that morning. Their family was wiped out financially, he said. For our family there was no inheritance left.

"Thank God we still have the business," said Mama. I'm glad we didn't know what was ahead.

CHAPTER 25

MOVING ON

A year or so after Papa died, Mama was ready to leave 301 East Capitol. There was nothing to keep her there.

After all, she wasn't a business woman. She was, as always, a singer. She had little connection with the business; none, really, except for the income and the signing of those huge sheets of blank checks.

Occasionally, I'd go downstairs to the office with her and watch as she put her name on dozens of pages of checks – six on each sheet. The business manager, who had started working for my father when he was 14 years old, always stood by the desk and watched, too.

Years later, I learned that domestic expenses, even mortgages, were paid (or not) with these checks. Such facts and figures couldn't have been of less interest to either Mama or me. At that time, that is.

So, leaving the running of the business to the businessmen, my mother and I explored Capitol Hill for a new place to live. Brother's interests were elsewhere in those years. He had become a student at St. Alban's, the Episcopal boys' school within the grounds of the Washington National Cathedral. He was driven there in his lower school years by the men who worked for the business.

At first, the house search was limited to East Capitol Street, and only as far as Lincoln Park.

My mother's first questions to the real estate agent were about the number of closets and bathrooms the house had. Our flat over the parlors had one clothes closet – a walled-off corner of the dining room – and one bathroom.

The rooms we looked at seemed huge, but, of course, they were empty and I'd never seen unfurnished houses before. Like the ladies from Boston who didn't buy hats because "we *have* our hats," the extended family I grew up in didn't poke around empty houses to move into. We *had* our houses, and in some cases, had had them for three, four, five generations. All on Capitol Hill.

Some of the houses we looked at seemed familiar, as if I had been there before. And, as I learned from my mother, I *had* been there. Many belonged to doctors who had died or moved away.

East Capitol Street was packed with doctors. And we had visited quite a few. This was the one where we had brought Aunt Addie when she had her "bilious attack." Two doors down had lived the doctor who treated Mama's migraines. Across the street was where we came with Aunt Gertie after she fell down Granny's cellar steps and broke her arm.

Providence Hospital was about five blocks from Granny's house, where these aunts lived. It would never have occurred to anyone to call an ambulance to take Aunt Gertie to the hospital. Nor did she go to an orthopedic surgeon. The doctor who set her arm (the wrist bone stuck out funny ever after) also delivered babies, and advised their apoplectic grandfathers to "cut back a bit."

There was a comforting social relationship between doctor and patient then that is often lost in today's sanitized medical system.

When we didn't feel well or had had an accident, we went to the doctor's house down the street for treatment. Or, if we were really sick, he (I didn't know there were female doctors until I was an adult) came to our house.

If one of our favorites, like Dr. Luce, was busy, we would call Dr. McQuillen (around on B Street, S.E.), and if he, too, was unavailable, Dr. Jaeger was just as good.

A doctor's visit to our home was as social as it was therapeutic. There was always time to chat over a piece of cake and a glass of sherry or Granny's blackberry wine. Or a stiff belt of straight whiskey. Medicinal. Especially in flu season, which could be in winter, spring, summer or fall.

I digress. Sorry.

We didn't buy a doctor's cast-off home after all. Instead, we leapfrogged over a goodly piece of the city and began inching our search up 16th Street, N.W.

Now we were in unknown territory. The farther out we went, the less the houses leaned on each other the way they did on Capitol Hill. They were standing alone, on bigger lots than I was used to, and they had low ceilings. A lot of them were light in color, which made them look lighter in bulk than the brownstones and the dark red brick I was familiar with.

One house that we inspected seemed especially alien to me. It was of Spanish design with Moorish touches, like the exotic fountain in a sort of courtyard. Beautiful, but I didn't feel at home there, and the sound of running water made me want to go to the bathroom.

This one, especially, was a long way from the Capitol dome just outside our living room window.

I was scared that it was the kind of house Mama would want, but she rejected it, as she had all the others, to my relief.

Around Memorial Day of 1927 (or was it 1926?) we packed our things and headed to Leonardtown for the summer. I thought that we also left behind plans for moving. I was wrong.

There must have been discussions, reviewing of architectural blueprints, buying furniture – all those things that occupy people who are about to move into a brand-new home. Whatever was happening on the adult level with respect to housing passed me by during that idyllic summer, as I lazed in the hammock or swung endlessly back and forth on my rope swing attached to a huge oak near the house, staring at Breton Bay.

As Labor Day approached, we packed again. This time, we were returning to 301 East Capitol – but only briefly, I discovered.

The "men downstairs" unpacked the car, with Brother's help, and we took off again. Mama looked smug, and refused to say more than, "It's a surprise."

Fred drove us for what seemed hours to a place as far from Capitol Hill as you can go and still be in D.C. Mama said to turn left at Kalmia, at just about the end of 16th Street N.W. then.

We wound for three or four blocks past impressive homes that didn't look like our type at all, then stopped when Mama uttered a piercing cry. It was not a cry of joy.

We had stopped in front of what I soon learned was our brand-new home – a dignified red brick colonial with white pillars rising two stories over the entry porch.

It was an understated thing of beauty, with no airs or pretense of grandeur, and bearing no resemblance whatever to the funeral parlors.

I warmed to it immediately.

The problem, in my mother's eyes, was that the house had been built at the edge of a steep terrace, and she saw it as teetering on the brink of the hill.

The builders, apparently on their own throughout the summer – no Zurhorsts on the site – dug into the hill and excavated for a two-car garage, then put one wing on top of the garage. The entryway and far wing followed logically at the top of the terrace.

Mama had pictured the whole thing set much farther back on the site. Actually, there wasn't room for the house back there. It was a big house, and the lot wasn't deep.

Just the same, for the next few months as the finishing touches were applied, she tried in every way possible to get the architect/contractor/stonemason/workman with a shovel – anyone who would listen – to move the house back 20 feet or so. Of course, none of them budged. Nor did the house.

Eventually, my mother reconciled herself to the inevitable, and we moved into the immovable house on the edge of a hill on Kalmia Road, directly opposite Rock Creek Park.

She never approached the house by car without a sad little shake of her head. If only she could push it back from the rim of the hill.

There were no flaws, however, with the warm, flowing and welcoming use of space within those walls.

This was Mama's dream house. And the heart of it was the music room, with its grand piano, which had been Aunt Mary's (she who gave us the alligator and baby lamb), and was the delight of Mama's soul. She reveled in the freedom to play it and sing her heart out without the restraint of "a body downstairs."

(She didn't count her effortless ability at the keyboard as a talent. That gift simply accompanied her voice.)

A very different kind of sound filled the house when my brother's band from St. Alban's lit up the little blue and gold music room.

I used to slink around the doorway just to get a glimpse of those gorgeous St. Alban's men, five years older than I, and from another world.

One unforgettable day after they had packed up their saxes and clarinets and put the drum set back in the basement rec room, they were gathered around the breakfast room table, having brownies and soda. While I adoringly watched them from a dark corner near the door, Bowdoin Craighill saw me and winked. Oh, ecstasy!

Mama loved to entertain, and this house gave her the chance to pull out all stops – the finest food, presented on the most elegant china, prepared by the master chef Weegie of St. Mary's County, and served with a certain *je ne sais quoi* by our handyman turned butler – Jeff.

When Mama was giving her dinner parties, Jeff loved nothing better than to play butler, dressed up in one of the swallowtail dress coats my grandfather wore as conductor of the orchestra at the National Theater. Grandpap was a small-boned slender man, at least six inches shorter than Jeff. No matter. Jeff stuffed himself into the coat, and, though unable to move his arms, managed to open the front door to the guests and usher them in, gesturing with hands just inches from his sides.

This butler act was not Mama's idea, but Jeff's own. In fact, at the initial dinner party, Jeff thrust a small silver tray into the hands of the first guest to arrive, and at the same time called out, "Miss Edwinetta, they's come!"

Later, he argued with Mama (Jeff and Granny had had a running argument going for at least forty years; he rarely argued with my mother) that he had served as butler more than she had ever imagined, and he knew that the butler presented a silver tray at the door, and then announced the arrivals. There was no mention of calling cards.

Since dinner parties at Kalmia were, indeed, elegant but informal, and small – rarely more than six invited guests – Mama let Jeff have his fun and play butler to the hilt. Weegie, too, enjoyed having full rein in her kitchen – choosing the menu and then preparing the meals with her unique skill. After dinner, she was usually invited into the dining room to accept the plaudits of the guests. She played her part with grace. And fully clothed.

Weegie's decision to come "up to the city" was a strange one. Sonny, her husband, was gone, and we were the only family she had.

She was delighted with her own room and bath – and radio – up the back stairway. The strange part was that she wanted no salary at all for three or four months, and then, when she was ready, she would be paid and given a ride back to Leonardtown, where she would go on a no-holds-barred binge for a week or so. She allowed herself another week to sober up before "calling for the limousine" as she termed this service. Then she'd return.

Weegie, in her own way, was only a bit more isolated in her room at the top of the back stairs than was the rest of the family, while we lived on Kalmia Road.

Even though on Capitol Hill we didn't socialize frequently, such as going to parties or running in and out of neighbors' houses, we knew they were there, up the street, or around the corner, or always in the same pew at St Mark's or St. Peter's. We were part of our neighborhood. And we had family around us. Even with their faults, we knew who they were, this Capitol Hill family and neighborhood.

Kalmia Road hadn't yet become a neighborhood. Maybe it never did. In our few years there I always felt it was a long way from home.

We were all the more cut off from the rest of the world because we didn't have a car at the house, and were nowhere near public transportation. Not that Mama or Granny would have taken a bus if it had stopped at the front door. And neither had ever learned to drive.

The men from the office drove that incredible distance across town from 301 to Kalmia to drive me back to St. Cecilia's for my last years there, and then to drive me from Kalmia to Gunston Hall for my first year at that high school.

Hermie, my friend from St. Cecilia's, and I used to talk on the phone frequently, but never visited. Well, to get from Anacostia across town to what was then the end of 16th Street, N.W., without a car, was like climbing Mt. Everest. It was out of the question.

My mother struck up a friendship with a neighbor who lived in a handsome house behind us. She was a charming woman, the wife of a Congressman from Ohio. He was a Republican.

I used to wonder what they talked about, if Mama's friend was a Republican. It was 1932, and Franklin Delano Roosevelt had just been elected President. All that we talked about in our house were Roosevelt's plans for action against the disastrous effects of the Depression (haunting pictures of starving men, women and children filled the newspapers); what he was going to do about wars and threats of wars hanging over Europe and the Far East; how he would handle Hitler, who was fast gaining power in Germany.

To me, it seemed as if everybody in a frightened world was rejoicing in the infectious confidence of the marvelous FDR. Everybody that I knew certainly was thrilled to have a new leader, a man we could trust.

Republicans, apparently, didn't trust him. I couldn't imagine how anyone could be a Republican in those times. Especially a close friend of my mother's.

So I made up my own scenario to suit my prejudice. In it, this nice lady was a closet Democrat who greatly admired FDR, but couldn't admit it because her husband was serving in Congress as a Republican.

That worked for me. I didn't tell my mother about it.

I almost had a friend of my own on Kalmia Road. A few weeks after we moved into the new house, a girl close to my age – nine or ten – came to the door with her mother.

The mother was apologetic, the girl shy. They had seen the movers bring in a doll house, said the mother, and, "I hope we're not intruding. We were wondering ... hoping ... that maybe you had a little girl?"

The mothers greeted each other enthusiastically. The girls less so. We just stared at each other while the mothers got acquainted over a cup of tea. They sent us off to play in the doll house which was in the dressing room off of one of the bedrooms. It was like trying to read a book together. It just didn't work.

After an awkward half hour or so, I suggested we go down to the kitchen and ask Weegie for some cookies. We ate them, and wondered what to do next. So we found our mothers in the den and went in and sat next to them. Very close.

"Did you girls have a lot of fun together?" asked the other mother cheerily.

The girl (I've forgotten her name) and I stared silently down at our Mary Jane shoes and looked embarrassed.

That was the only time I saw her. I often wondered if she was looking out of her window just as I was, in hopes of catching a glimpse, having another go at it. It might have worked the second time. But we didn't even try.

We hadn't been living in the house very long before a pattern set in on weekends. Aunt Leila and Aunt Rita would catch a ride with our driver on Friday after he picked me up at St. Cecilia's. They would spend the weekend on Kalmia Road and go back Monday morning.

These were Schroeder great-aunts from 524 Ninth Street – my mother's father's sisters.

On alternate weekends Aunt Emmie and Aunt Daisy rode to the house for the three-night visit. They were also from 524 Ninth Street, the Schroeder house. Except that Aunt Daisy wasn't a Schroeder at all. She had been a friend of another one of my grandfather's sisters, and used to visit the household. Then she became a *very* good friend of Aunt Emmie's, and moved in.

She never went back to Frostburg or Hagerstown or wherever she was from.

And Aunt Leila and Aunt Rita stopped speaking to Aunt Emmie and Aunt Daisy forevermore. Even though they lived in the same little house together for many years.

I benefitted the most from the social arrangement, because each pair of visitors lavished gifts on me each weekend. Aunt Rita proudly had been a saleslady at the Fine Jewelry Department at Woodward and Lothrop's Department Store for many years. Aunt Daisy was a saleslady at the rival Hecht's in downtown D.C.

Although I didn't get any fine jewelry, the lively competition between the stores – personified by the two "aunts," each with her own store discount – resulted in some of the most luxuriant satin nightgowns, peignoirs and lingerie of any little girl or grown-up lady on Kalmia Road.

Sometimes now when an old movie shows up on TV, I recognize a glamorous nightie or dressing gown on Gloria Swanson or Joan Crawford, and I can smugly claim, "Just like one I had."

Nobody believes me.

These aunts, in their 50s and 60s at that time, had lived all of their lives in a house without indoor plumbing. So their greatest pleasure was visiting each of the six or seven facilities at our house at least once each day of their stay.

As soon as Brother became 16, he got a car – an irresistibly cute Ford roadster with a rumble seat perched on the rear end.

That addition to the family made all the difference to *him,* of course. But it also delighted the rest of us.

We used it more for pleasure than for practical errands.

Our favorite place to go was the Hot Shoppe down on Georgia Avenue in D.C., the first of the vast Marriott empire to come.

We would drive into the parking lot and sidle up to a call box much like the drive-throughs today. The driver gave the order, and soon it was delivered on a tray that attached to the driver's side door.

I always ordered "minced beef barbecue, no slaw, root beer."

No barbecue since has achieved the perfection of the early Hot Shoppes minced beef barbecue sandwich served on a rectangular bun made for the sole purpose of complementing the contents. And available nowhere else.

One warm evening, Mama cajoled Brother into taking us for a ride in Rock Creek Park. The park started for our family just across the street from the Kalmia Road house.

Mama claimed her favorite spot – the rumble seat. I jumped in next to her for this spin in the park. Granny was in front next to Brother.

We were slowly wending our way down Beach Drive when a scruffy, wild-haired figure appeared, walking along the side of the road.

As we drew near him, the man stopped and turned toward us. Mama waved.

He beamed her a luminous smile, and, raising his hand in a gesture worthy of a papal benediction, he called out gently, "Shit," and waved us around the next curve.

For the next few years, whenever Mama burst into convulsive laughter for no obvious reason, I knew the source.

I laughed with her, though I didn't have any idea what the word meant. I finally asked Brother, and, of course, he knew.

How do big brothers know things like that? Does someone tell them, or do they just ... know?

We had few uninvited visitors, so it was a surprise when a cab stopped in front of the house, and a tall, distinguished white-haired gentleman got out. I was hanging out in the music room, listening to Mama sing some German *Lieder*.

"Somebody's coming up the front steps," I said.

She joined me at the window. Neither of us recognized the well-dressed stranger making his way slowly up the long flight of brick stairs that curved up to the entrance.

Mama opened the door as he ceremoniously removed his grey fedora. "You must be Edwinetta," he said. "I'm your cousin John Sanderson. I hope I'm not intruding."

As we had tea in the living room before an open fire, he explained where he was "perched on the family tree," as he put it.

He belonged somewhere among the Sheltons, the Sandersons, Tydings, Watkins, that lot. Granny's English side of the family.

After an hour or so he asked Mama to call him a cab to take him back to his home in Chevy Chase. He made these impromptu visits every two or three months during the fall and winter. In the summer, of course, we were in Leonardtown, and didn't see him.

Then he just stopped coming. Mama telephoned him, but couldn't reach him.

We realized, after the visits ended, that we had grown fond of his formal, proper manners, his elegant presence, though we never really got to know him. He was like Hamlet's father's ghost – unreal, not meant to last long on the stage. Unforgettable, just the same.

Cousin John belonged in the make-believe world of our lovely Kalmia Road house. Life wasn't quite real there, not in the way that Capitol Hill was real.

⚬⚬

Reality broke in on the dream one night in 1931, with a phone call from Hermie, my friend from St. Cecilia's.

"Have you heard?" She was breathless. "The Japanese ... or maybe it's the Chinese ... anyway, they've invaded Manchuria! And listen to this ... they tore down the American flag!"

"They tore down the *American flag*?" It seemed forever before either of us could say anything appropriate for such an act. Then I asked her where Manchuria was.

"I don't know," she whispered.

Strange that we two should be so terrified by something happening so far away – wherever Manchuria was. But this news from an alien land hit us like a bolt of lightning, streaking out of dark, distant storm clouds.

They had been hovering there, ominous, threatening, for a long time. The world knew a storm was coming, but when would it break? And where? And how?

Was this the beginning? The beginning of what?

By tearing down the American flag, some foreign foe in Asia had, in that instant for Hermie and me, destroyed the invulnerability of the American flag and "the republic for which it stands."

Maybe now our country would have to go to war, we both thought, though we didn't speak of the unspeakable.

In a war, did everybody die?

All that we girls at Gunston Hall High School knew about war was what we learned in the classroom. And at that time – the early Thirties – we were studying ancient history, and falling in love (this was a girls' school) with Alexander the Great.

Our Social Sciences teacher, Miss Spear, was trying to acquaint us with "the gathering storm" through the newspapers, but at first the problems seemed far away and unrelated to our lives.

Then one day, Miss Spear, wide-eyed, told us, "Adolph Hitler has been elected Chancellor of Germany."

We knew who Hitler was. When we went to the movies, the newsreels before the main feature were full of scenes of stiff-legged and stiff-armed soldiers goose-stepping across the screen and shouting, "Heil Hitler!"

They looked so ridiculous that we young movie goers used to laugh at them. And later the humongous choruses singing stirring, martial music at these rallies surpassed any massed choirs we had ever heard. They were – I admit – thrilling.

But at the moment when Miss Spear made her announcement, something in her eyes, something in her bearing, sent a current of fear down our spines. The goose-stepping wasn't funny any more. The silly little mustache was no longer something to giggle at.

Here was another danger signal breaking out of the darkening skies of the early Thirties. Only this time the charge was coming from the other side of the world, Europe.

Then even worse news hit us, right at home. The telephone call came for my mother. It was a male voice. He sounded drunk, she said. After some verbal abuse, he told her that the family was wiped out financially – the business deep in debt, mortgages on both the Leonardtown house and the Kalmia Road house unpaid.

His parting shot was for her to get ready for the poor house. When she hung up the phone, her whole body was quivering.

The message was soon verified. We had little left. What had happened to those endless pages of checks Mama used to sign each month? High-powered, high-priced lawyers couldn't tell us, and neither could anybody else. We had no answers.

Within a few months of the dramatic call, my mother had a massive stroke. She died, at home, less than three hours later. She was 42.

Granny, as always, was an anchor for our emotions. At 14, I continued going to Gunston Hall, though in a sort of fog. Brother, who was 18, left college – St. John's, Annapolis – to take over the business and save it from bankruptcy. He suddenly became a man, and a very competent one.

Thanks to his efforts, the business did not go bankrupt.

And another Good Thing happened. In the midst of sorrow at my mother's death, along with incomprehensible financial disaster (were we left with *no money at all?*), Brother and I took the train to Chicago to see the 1933 World's Fair. I don't remember much about the fair itself.

All I remember – and please, don't mention this to anybody, especially Granny – all I remember is a dancer named Sally Rand, who did something called a Fan Dance in a theater. She had tremendous, pastel-colored fans that she kept waving about, keeping her completely covered. Most of her, most of the time. Honestly.

There were lovely soft lights and soft music that put me right to sleep. Brother, for some reason, stayed wide awake. We saw the show several times.

Brother said he'd make me really sorry if I told anybody. So please ... there wasn't really anything naughty about the fan dance. Honest. Anyway, by then I was 14, which is old enough ... don't you think? Just don't say anything to Granny. Brother'd kill me.

The two households – Granny's two surviving sisters from 318 A Street, S.E., and Granny and Brother and I – joined and moved into a large house on Longfellow Street, N.W. Weegie returned to Leonardtown, ready to go home.

After a couple of years, Brother, now the head of the family, announced that we couldn't afford the $100 per month rent any longer, and once more we packed up and moved.

This time, we were back to Square One: over the parlors at 301 East Capitol.

It was a comfort to have the Capitol so close once again. But otherwise, returning to our old, cramped quarters seemed like a defeat. We thought we had escaped from the funeral parlors.

Now we were in a different family configuration: Aunt Kate had died on Longfellow Street, so only Aunt Gertie came with us, along with Granny, of course.

Life settled into a dull routine of high school classes, homework, searches for lost books and papers and assignments and even shoes – make that *one* shoe. I always seemed to be missing just one shoe. The mid-30's turned into a hectic, frantic, utterly disorganized time.

For fun, I watched funerals leave the building.

And so I accepted with *pleasure* an invitation to dinner at the home of a couple who had known my parents through a musical connection.

Miss Elsa, as I was told to call her, was a pianist. A bloodless pianist who never struck a wrong note. Mr. John was a tall, muscular man who worked in a nameless office.

The dinner went off without incident, but it soon turned into a weekly obligation for dinner every Thursday at 6 p.m. *promptly*.

That commitment became nightmarish within a few weeks. After dinner one night, Mr. John turned on a shortwave radio that crackled and squawked but still aired the voice of a man with a cultured British accent who called himself "Lord Haw Haw."

In disbelief, I heard him talk about the purification of the Aryan race that was to be accomplished by eliminating all non-Aryans, especially Jews. He also marked for destruction all gypsies, many Slavic people, and "defectives and other undesirables."

At the end of the program, Mr. John sprang to his feet, and, very erect, extended his arm in the Nazi salute.

"Sieg Heil!" he shouted in unison with the speaker. "Heil Hitler!"

I sat very still, wanting to bolt out the door but too frightened to move. "What you have just heard is the wave of the future," said Mr. John, his eyes boring into mine.

That evening in the streetcar going back to East Capitol Street, I felt that everybody around me could tell that I had become part of something foul, some unspeakable evil that would take over the world and everybody in it.

I told no one what was happening. But with increasing fear, I returned the next Thursday. And the next Thursday after that.

After listening to Lord Haw Haw, my hosts would inform me of the plans outlined in Hitler's *Mein Kampf.* "Today Germany; tomorrow the world," Mr. John often quoted. Miss Elsa showed me pictures of relatives back in "The Fatherland," where their parents had come from. I was told that before der Fuhrer came to power, these people, now smiling and waving swastika flags beside their new cars, had been destitute, out of work, hungry. But Hitler had greatly improved the economy – in dire straits since the nation's defeat in World War I – by building its industrial strength, she said, and by advancing such massive projects as the autobahn.

One Thursday, after a particularly venomous attack on the Jewish people by Lord Haw Haw, Mr. John complained about having to "rub shoulders with them and other filthy scum" as he rode the streetcar to work.

At that moment I knew there was no gracious way to end the relationship. I had to get out of there. "I'm sorry," I muttered, as I grabbed my coat and ran out the door.

I never saw them again.

But I did hear from them, through a great aunt who also knew the couple. Miss Elsa had called her to report on my "shocking rudeness." And Aunt Susie reprimanded me for being "disrespectful to people who had been so kind" to me.

My regret is that I listened to such inhumanity for so many weeks without protesting. Why did it take so long for the horror to set in? Though it's no excuse, I'm aware all these years later that I was not the only one in the world with inexcusably delayed outrage. But how could I have stayed silent?

Meanwhile, my brother had acquired a lovely wife, and they moved into the second apartment in the building – the one that occasionally had rats. The former manager of the firm used to occupy it with his family.

Esther May, the new member of the clan, had won immediate approval from Granny and her sisters when Brother introduced her to them on the porch at Longfellow Street.

As she came up the porch steps, three rocking chairs came to a halt, as three pairs of eyes gazed past her lovely face and down to her trim ankles. Three heads nodded acceptance.

She was wearing stockings. Silk stockings.

Here was a worthy mate for the young man they had doted on since he was born 21 years before.

The other dates he had brought home had come with bare legs. A social *faux pas* to the aunts and Granny. Nylons had not yet been invented, and silk hose were expensive and had a seam down the back that always went crooked. The social misfits who wore lisle stockings looked dreadful when these hose bunched around the ankles, as they always did. And they were hot. It was summertime. (I had three or four pair, of course.)

Esther May brought joy into our lives. She also became the sister I had always wanted. With her there, the parlors became less funereal, and even, at times, fun.

A year or so later, things got even better at 301: Esther May and Brother produced a wonderful baby boy – another Charles Stewart Zurhorst, who lightened the lives of all of us beyond measure.

By now, Brother had accomplished what he set out to do: the business was on a firm footing financially. It was too late to save the house in Leonardtown and the one on Kalmia. The banks had foreclosed.

But the funeral home that had been established in 1868 had survived with honor.

Looking at his small son, my brother saw a fifth generation Zurhorst who seemed destined to claim the business as his heritage. Was running a funeral home the career this child would want?

The last two men who had been in charge – my brother and his father – had disliked it. Now was the time to break the chain before another life was sacrificed to family loyalty and obedience. He made a decision without looking back: Sell the business.

After he put the firm on the market, he found that the Zurhorst name was the most valuable asset of all. So he sold the Zurhorst name to the new owner (a good and honorable man) to use in a business sense.

And that was that.

We said goodbye to the parlors with no regrets, and headed for Montgomery County, Maryland – Falkland Apartments, to be exact, at 16th Street and East-West Highway. Granny and I in one apartment (Aunt Gertie was now gone); Brother, Esther May, and "Colt" in another less than a block away.

By 1939, I was a junior at Maryland University, with my own convertible – named "Belle."

Brother was in public relations and script-writing at a D.C. radio station.

We had cut our ties to Capitol Hill. Or so we thought.

CHAPTER 26

BACK TO CAPITOL HILL

As I picked up a newly fallen horse chestnut, I looked at the Capitol Dome above me and silently sent a message: "I'm home again." It was 1968.

Two young squirrels scurried past me, chasing each other into the cool shade of the Olmsted summer house.

Since the ancestors of these creatures had played around my feet almost 40 years before, I had graduated from college, written print ads for Woodward and Lothrop's Department Store (RIP), then had become writer/editor of *Broadcasting Magazine,* married, had a fine daughter and son, divorced, and somehow landed as a speechwriter in the Kennedy-Johnson White House, in early September 1963.

Just three months before Dallas.

I stayed on, writing for the Johnson Administration, and then for the next three Presidents, as staff writer for a committee that reported directly to the President but was housed within the Department of Health, Education & Welfare (now Health & Human Services).

The best part of that job was not the White House connection, but the Capitol connection. My office was at the base of Capitol Hill, on the west side. Better yet, I was transported by train – a real choo-choo train – from picturesque Kensington, Maryland, near my home, to Union Station, a couple of short blocks from the Capitol and its grounds.

From the moment Kenny, the conductor, yelled, "All aboard!" until we arrived at the station about a half hour later, every minute was pure pleasure.

Early on, I just looked for an empty seat and took it when I found one. Gradually, I searched for backs of heads that had become familiar, and hoped for an empty seat next to one of them. As time went on, more and more hands waved, and faces turned, inviting me to join them.

Few places offered a higher intellectual level of companionship than the train that had come down the tracks from Brunswick, Maryland, picking up the cream of the crop along the way. It was a prime conveyor for staffers on many levels who worked "on the Hill," and at the Supreme Court, Library of Congress, Folger Shakespeare Library, plus HEW and Housing & Urban Development.

When we stopped at Forest Glen, we could overlook the Capital Beltway, far below us. It was always teeming with cars.

"Poor devils," we would commiserate, while feeling deliciously superior and relaxed in our rail car. This ritual was especially satisfying in nasty weather. We lorded it over the poor souls below. How petty. How disgusting. How delightful.

One morning in the early 1970s, a seatmate asked if I knew that a Senator was now riding our train.

I had, indeed, heard the news.

Nobody knew who it was, but we made bets on several new faces.

Eventually – after a few weeks – I had our Senator pegged: Heavy-set. Jowls. Flowing silver hair. Sixtyish. Despite the fact that he was unsenatorially silent, we – my train pals and I – decided that he was the one, and the speculation died out.

There were lots of snow birds on the train one morning. (Snow birds rode with us only in bad weather.) Just one seat was empty in my usual car. It was located in that cluster of four seats at the end of the car, now occupied by three men I didn't know. The loud-mouth next to me was blowing off about "damned politicians." He had nothing good to say about elected officials of either party. "They're all a bunch of crooks." The two men across from us remained stoically silent.

But as we were pulling into the train yard of Union Station, I couldn't keep my own loud mouth shut one more minute. I let the ignoramus have it.

In less than ladylike terms, I told him what I thought of the garbage he had been spewing about politicians. And gratuitously added my pleasure that he was not counted among them. To his annoyance, I lectured him about the power that each member of Congress wields – and the admiration due those who resist the temptation to abuse it. There are more than we realize.

The timing was providential, since the train came to a stop just as I cited the unequalled political rhetoric of Adlai Stevenson, Democratic Presidential candidate in 1952 and 1956: Politics, he often said (more or less), is not inherently good or evil. The word political comes from the Greek *politicos* – of the citizens. In short, politicians are us.

I found myself even pronouncing the word in the Stevenson manner: "poe-lit-ical." His respect for the term had forever lifted politics above the level of smoke-filled back rooms for me and raised it to a position of honor in our democracy.

We were leaving the car when I noticed that the man who had sat opposite me was behind me now, gently trying to get my attention.

He smiled, looking slightly embarrassed.

"I never heard anybody taking up for politicians like that," he said. And we easily fell into a conversation about politics and politicians as we walked through the newly refurbished Union Station and turned toward the east side of the Capitol.

Actually, my office was in the opposite direction, but I didn't want to interrupt the good talk we were having.

So we continued on to the Old Senate Office Building, avoiding the trash cans with "Old SOB" stenciled on their sides, lined up at the curb. (There were two office buildings for the Senators then, known, as I remember them, as the Old SOB and across First Street, the New SOB. Now we have the Russell, the Dirksen and the Hart, and there isn't a joke among them.)

As I split off to take my usual route through the Capitol grounds, he asked where I worked. I told him and asked the same question of him.

"On the Hill," he answered.

With a wave, he called out, "I'll probably see you tonight on the train."

Sure enough, there he was on the homebound train, standing beside a seat he had saved for me. I figured he was in his early 40s, trim, with sandy, dark blond hair. A nice, decent guy.

After inquiring about my work and my family, he listened with genuine interest as I told him.

He described his wife and children with touching pride, and even threw in a few remarks about the house they had recently moved into, in a lovely, tree-shaded community, one train stop before mine.

In the beginning, he didn't talk much about his work.

But one night a few weeks after we had met, I found him guarding a pair of empty seats on the train, waving me up the aisle.

He was eager to tell me that he had unexpectedly been interviewed on TV the night before. Modest and unpretentious as he was, he was excited about this event.

And though I had been suspicious, now I was sure. This was the mystery Senator on the train. The secret was out.

Over the next 30 years he became one of the most respected and powerful men to serve in the Senate. He was Pete Domenici (R-N.Mex).

The Senator and I had many more amiable chats on our commute, but I never again walked him to the Old SOB. That route took me four or five blocks out of my way to work.

Something I had noticed earlier, however, gave me an idea. The less than auspicious back door of the Old SOB (now Russell Senate Office Building), by being at ground level, seemed so accessible that it almost invited visitors to enter. Remember, this was the early 70s. Don't try it today. Or you'll be sorry.

The door was open, and I decided to explore – to see if I could find an underground passage through the Old Senate Office Building to the Capitol basement, then over to the House Office Buildings, still tunneling, and finally out at the base of the Capitol Hill's West Side, through the Rayburn HOB garage.

Once safely past the casual identity check at the door of the Old SOB, I was committed to the adventure. To my surprise, I found signs in the form of a hand, drawn with the index finger pointing, marked Tunnel. Or did it say Capitol? Or Exit? To the Lions, maybe?

I've forgotten what they said, but they steered me through connecting underground tunnels, down stairs, up elevators, through long, dark passages, and under gigantic pipes hugging the low ceilings.

The hissing of steam filled some parts of the tunnel, while just ahead, sizzling bacon and an unexpected short-order lunch counter added a human touch.

There were so many turns and curves and ups and downs that I lost all sense of direction in those corridors. The passage was never empty. People were working down there, mixing paints, checking loud machinery, hammering, doing repairs in a carpentry shop, frying eggs, copying papers, monitoring security cameras and stacking crates marked THIS END UP.

The most fun in the busy labyrinth below ground was riding the subway cars – one set connecting with the Senate Office Buildings, the other leading to the House Office Buildings. They used to be open to the public.

There was priority seating, of course, for members of Congress of both Houses, when a roll-call vote had been called. Then, bells rang, and Senators and Representatives came rushing out of the hallways leading to the rails that ran to the Capitol.

Now visitors must be accompanied by a staffer, understandably. I have a tender memory of riding this subway (much older version) with my children when they were little, to begin their acquaintance with the Capitol. They loved those toy-like cars as much as I did.

In my 1970s trek through the underground passage, I finally ended up in the Rayburn Building garage, a short walk from my office.

I felt as if I had scaled the dome. Even better, I now knew more about the intimate details of daily life in the Capitol than ever before – where they stored their junk, old paint cans, broken chairs, and daily garbage. Here was the down-to-earth underbelly of the Capitol. I loved it.

My discovery remained a secret, even from close friends on the train. And so, one evening when a heavy storm broke just as I started walking from my office to Union Station, I ducked into the Rayburn garage and made my way through the underground passage all the way back to the rear door of the Russell Senate Office Building. By the time I came out, the storm had ended, though the ground was still wet. My fellow commuters were also wet. Soaked, in fact.

They pelted me with questions.

"Why are you dry?" "How did you do that?"

I answered with an enigmatic smile. It is very satisfying to be an insider, even on the lowest level. And even if it takes almost a lifetime to achieve the honor.

Early one crisp, clear morning, I emerged from Union Station into a blast of frigid air that was snapping bare branches and sweeping the clouds away.

The great dome of the Capitol, directly ahead, sparkled as its windows caught the slanted rays of the winter sun.

Suddenly, the couple in front of me stopped abruptly. They were a Norman Rockwell pair – rounded, smallish, pink-cheeked. No longer young.

He put down the two suitcases he was carrying, looked up, and with one quick gesture removed his knitted cap and held it against his heart.

"Good God, ma," he said, with reverence. "There it is."

Glory, glory, hallelujah!

ACKNOWLEDGEMENTS

This book began to come to life about four years ago, unbidden, but it never would have survived without the help of some wonderful friends.

Leading the list is John Franzén, whose personal and professional guidance lighted my way on every page. And even before John entered the picture there was Laetitia Yeandle, urging friends in the Ruth Ann Overbeck Capitol Hill History Project to interview a "cave dweller" – me. The Overbeck volunteers, Maygene Daniels and Bernadette McMahon, never got their recorded interview, but thanks to their interest and encouragement, a book began to emerge from my typewriter. (I have never yet found a user-friendly computer.)

Maygene and Bernadette kept encouraging, and the pages kept coming. Their patient husbands Steve Daniels and Jim McMahon also turned cheerleaders when my cheer ran out, and Jim used his considerable knowledge of the Library of Congress to aid in the book's progress.

Then came Gail Dearing Price, who whisked parts of the manuscript to California where she transcribed them into digital form. More of the book was transcribed by Kathy Trotter, Vivianne and Elliot Pierce, Joe Ryan and his daughter Hannah, plus the Big Surprise, Melissa Hampton, a complete stranger, who drove a great distance to volunteer her services as a transcriber. She's the world's fastest, and no longer a stranger.

Professional knowledge and first-rate research were gifts from the United States Marine Band's librarian Mike Ressler, Capitol grounds superintendent Ted Bechtol, and U.S. Senate historian Donald Richie. Each went out of his way to be helpful, and I'm grateful.

My first readers slogged through an early draft and egged me on. This was a task more for family and close friends than for professional proofreaders and critics, and they did it magnificently. My most profound thanks to Sister Miriam John of the Cross, O.C.D., whose ability to find anything on-line struck me as miraculous. There were many advisors and encouragers: Gail Blaufarb, Susanna Gray, Roger Gray, Charles Zurhorst, Craig Zurhorst (whose enthusiasm was a shot in the arm), Dave Blaufarb, Mary Kay Krump, Susan Walker, Kirsten Free, Jean West, and *Cul de Sac* cartoonist Richard Thompson. Thanks also to first-class photographer Alice Jackson and to Nancy Freeman, who deftly restored my faded family photos.

Many of the other contributors to this book don't fit into any one category of gratitude. They know what they did: John Davis, Teresa Wren, Nancy Block, Dee Washington, Ruth Aspron, Ismael Sanchez, Tom Tappan, Cindy Janke, Rosemary Freeman, the Willard Hotel's Barbara Bahny, the National Theatre's John Loomis, authors Aleck Loker, Tom Allen and Norman Polmar, and DC transportation expert Harry Gates. I am indebted to Carlton Fletcher for almost all of the material about my Aunt Mary's professional career.

Thank you to Ryan Grenier for his faith in the book even before the first chapter was completed. There are no words that could express my gratitude to *The Post*'s Michael Ruane and to my dear Key West cousin Linda Carter.

And what a joy to be welcomed back on a visit to 301 East Capitol by the "Folger folk" who now own it – the return arranged by my great pen pal, Stephen Grant. As he worked on a book about the Folgers of 201 East Capitol, I worked on a book about the Zurhorsts of 301 East Capitol … with a lot of help from my friends.

Bless 'em, every one!

Especially John Franzén.

Mary Z. Gray
July 4, 2011

ABOUT THE AUTHOR

Mary Z. Gray was born into a Capitol Hill family in 1919 and grew up above their inherited funeral parlors, two blocks from the U.S. Capitol. Since the 1840s the extended family had lived in, and rarely moved out of, a ten-block area of the neighborhood.

A writer all of her adult life, she got her first byline in *The Washington Post* in 1940. Since then, she has been published frequently in *The Post*, as well as *The New York Times* Travel Section and many other U.S. and Canadian papers. In the 1940s she was a reporter/editor for *Broadcasting Magazine*.

She became a speech writer for the Kennedy-Johnson White House in 1963 and continued as a writer for a Presidential committee for the next 14 years. In this period she also wrote speeches for Cabinet members and members of Congress.

Her book *Ah Bewilderness! Muddling Through Life With Mary Z. Gray* (Atheneum) was published in 1984.

A resident of Silver Spring, Maryland, since 1939, she has a son and daughter, a grandson, and three great-grandchildren.

This book was inspired by conversations with members of the Ruth Ann Overbeck Capitol Hill History Project.